Ken Ulmer is one of America's new voices, rising with a penetrating call to pragmatic spiritual dynamics. As a Christian leader, he stands tall; as a servant to society, he stands out; as a friend, he stands trustworthy; as a man of God, he stands close—in touch with our Father, that he might be in touch with Him whose touch can change the world.

—Jack W. Hayford
Chancellor/Pastor, The King's Seminary
The Church on the Way
Van Nuys, California

My dear friend, Bishop Kenneth Ulmer, is one of the most outstanding, creative preachers of our time. In *The Anatomy of God,* he has given us a creative, biblical treasure that will not only capture our minds, but will also move our hearts toward a God whose heart is moved toward us. Reading this book will compel you to love God more deeply and to worship Him more fully!

—Dr. Crawford W. Loritts, Jr.
Speaker, Author, Radio Host
Associate Director, Campus Crusade for Christ

In *The Anatomy of God,* Bishop Kenneth Ulmer reveals from Scripture just how completely and fantastically our great God and Savior loves and cares for us, illuminating facets of His being that many believers have no doubt never considered.

—Dr. Bill Bright
Founder of Campus Crusade for Christ

# The Anatomy of GOD

## BISHOP KENNETH ULMER

WHITAKER
HOUSE

**THE ANATOMY OF GOD**

Kenneth C. Ulmer
333 West Florence Ave.
Inglewood, CA 90301

ISBN: 0-88368-711-9
Printed in the United States of America
© 2001 by Kenneth C. Ulmer

Whitaker House
30 Hunt Valley Circle
New Kensington, PA 15068

Library of Congress Cataloging-in-Publication Data

Ulmer, Kenneth C.
  The anatomy of God / by Kenneth Ulmer.
     p. cm.
Includes bibliographical references.
  ISBN 0-88368-711-9 (pbk. : alk. paper)
  1. God—Attributes. I. Title.
  BT130 .U56 2002
  231'.4—dc21                                      2001008172

1 2 3 4 5 6 7 8 9 10 11 12 13 14 / 11 10 09 08 07 06 05 04 03 02

# Contents

# One

# Anatomically Speaking

Father, I want to know Thee, but my coward heart fears to give up its toys. I cannot part with them without inward bleeding, and I do not try to hide from Thee the terror of the parting. I come trembling, but I do come. Please root from my heart all those things which I have cherished so long and which have become a very part of my living self, so that Thou mayest enter and dwell there without a rival. Then shalt Thou make the place of Thy feet glorious. Then shall my heart have no need of the sun to shine in it, for Thyself will be the light of it, and there shall be no night there.
—A. W. Tozer, *The Pursuit of God*

The scene is not an uncommon one. Midnight has ticked by long ago, and everyone in my house is asleep but me. I am cocooned in my office wondering if tomorrow's— now *today's*—sermon will miraculously appear before I have to "exegete" the text to pieces. It never does, and I must confess I really don't mind. For you see, it is in these still hours that I allow my one true obsession to take flight. I pore over Scripture, dissect related material, and peek through a myriad of windows adorning the latest Bible study software, to the end that I might catch a new glimpse of *Him*.

*"I beseech thee, show me thy glory"* (Exodus 33:18). Moses was more than merely curious when he asked for the Lord's visible presence on Mount Sinai. And although I don't presume to claim that mighty prophet's "friendship" with God, I have at times been powerless to control the begging of my own soul to see more of the One who cannot be contained by heaven and earth. I am the psalmist's hart, panting for just a sip, just a taste, of something I can't live without. It has been the most fruitful pursuit of my life. I have never been disappointed. All attempts to fathom our unfathomable Father are rewarded with equal amounts of harvest and hunger. I continuously seek Him, even as I luxuriate in what I have found.

I've been doing this for quite a few years now, and I realized something long ago—God enjoys this as much as I do. He's not being coy with me. He's not playing "hard to get." He wants me to chase Him. In fact, He's egging me on. He wants to be "caught." Ours is a game in which we both win every time I get another look at Him. Second Corinthians 3:18 says the more we see Him, the more we mirror who He is. In other words, each glimpse means more glory to His name.

If, then, it is our view of God that grows us and changes us, we can only conclude that where there is no growth, or where there is inhibited growth, the view has been obstructed. Knowing this, I struggle sometimes as a pastor when I see people coming to church Sunday in and Sunday out, seeming to seek the Lord and seeming never to find Him. I know I'm not the only shepherd who feels like he's ladling out way too much milk to folks who should be chewing on steak by now.

It can't be God's fault. Every act, every thought, every motive of God is rooted in the deepest desire of His heart, which is to be known. His Word, from Genesis to Revelation, is a divine detailing of who He is. Every man, woman, account, and proverb therein adds another line, shade, color, or contour to His magnificent canvas. The signs and wonders He performed in the Holy Scriptures, as well as the ones He's still performing in our everyday lives, are not just stunts executed to impress us. He doesn't need our approval or applause. They were not even done so that men would believe, but rather that men would know *whom* they believe. Every prophet, angel, apostle, and teacher in the Bible had one assignment: to proclaim or project His personhood. And today, every evangelist, pastor, minister, and Christian author or artist has that same mandate. John 1:3 says, *"All things were made by him; and without him was not any thing made that was made."* Of course, that means that He made everything. But I would suggest to you that it also means that He's *in* everything, which means that all of God's creation, all of His handiwork, tells us something about Him. All things created help us see the Creator.

> Every act, every thought, every motive of God is rooted in the deepest desire of His heart, which is to be known.

The Father's most obvious effort at self-revelation can be found in our own mirrors. Of course, He is not flesh and blood. He is, as Jesus told the woman at the well, a Spirit. He is omnipresent, omnipotent, omniscient, and holy. And that's just the punctuation on His calling card. So God does not have a body per se. In fact, nowhere in the Bible is there a reference to the body of God. The closest representation of that is the body of Christ, Christ the Messiah, God incarnate, or God in the flesh. The Bible does not speak of God's having a body. But we do find numerous mentions of specific body parts. Now that doesn't mean He is a collection of disjointed ghostly limbs, organs, and features floating around in the cosmos. It means that God has chosen to reveal Himself to us in concepts and ideas that we can understand. Our own anatomy is God's most complete biography of Himself. It's as though He uses our bodies to play a kind of spiritual game of *Where's Waldo?* with us. In the midst of a world filled with visible, audible, tangible, mental, palatal, and olfactory options between good and evil, the clearest look we can get at Him is literally right under our noses. Our Father, whose mercy and kindness abound toward us always, created man in such a fashion that we, in the finitude and limitations of our humanity, are capable of visualizing and ultimately comprehending our infinite and limitless God. We were designed so that God could teach us about Himself.

> Our own anatomy is God's most complete biography of Himself.

In this book, we're going to look at the anatomy of God. We're going to try to understand the person and nature of God by looking at what He says about Himself in physiological and physical terms. We are using a theological and literary device called anthropomorphism. Now that's just a ten-cent word you can cut in half to make two five-cent words that make sense. *Anthrop* or *anthros* means "of or pertaining to man." *Morphism* means "form" or "shape." So to say that we're going to see God in anthropomorphic terms simply means we'll see Him in the form of man, or in human terms. Just consider it man's label for something God decided to do while man was still a pile of dust on the floor of Eden.

## An Invitation to Intimacy

Over the years, I have received literally thousands of invitations to banquets, weddings, fund-raisers, awards dinners, and various other events. I look at the information relevant to my schedule and commitments, then I make a determination about whether or not I'll be able to attend. I don't think about it much further than that. But my wife can often tell, just by looking at the invitation, what kind of gathering it will be. I know where to be and what time to show up. She can tell from the paper stock, the ink, the wording on the card, and the quality of the lettering on the envelope if we can expect succulent filets and delicate confections or rubbery chicken and boxed cake. I count on her to tell me if I'm dressed inappropriately. If we're expected to make a donation, she has the checkbook. She is seldom surprised at these things. (I, on the other hand, think some invitations should come with disclaimers so I'm not caught off guard. Something like, "Event will actually be more tedious and less significant than it appears on this invitation" would be most helpful. Or, "We advise eating a good meal before coming to this luncheon if bad food is not to your liking." What I'd really like to see, though, is this: "We planned to start on time, but our plans won't be working out at this affair.")

A lot more could be known about an event and the people putting it on if more attention were paid to the invitation. That said, I want you to consider that the Bible is a divinely written invitation to eternal fellowship with the Almighty. God drafted it personally through almost 40 human authors, in 66 volumes, 1,189 chapters, 31,173 verses, and 774,746 words. No expense was spared on this invitation. Jesus Christ gave His life to deliver it to you. Moses, Isaiah, David, John, Paul, Jeremiah, Daniel, and so many others became living pens through which the Holy Spirit extended the Father's request for the pleasure of your company.

I mention this here because I want you to understand as we study the Word of God within these pages that God's pursuit of you has been a deliberate and methodical act of grace. He did not save you to take you to heaven to keep Him company. He is not lonely. You're not doing Him any favors when you worship Him. His chest doesn't stick out any farther because you thank Him. He'd still be awesome if you didn't praise Him. He would exist in all His glory even if you didn't believe in Him. If you don't understand the complete lack of need for you on God's part, you might miss the wonder of your salvation. You might miss how utterly in love with you God is if you think His motive for saving you was selfish in any way. And if you see His love for you as anything less than perfect, you know Him as less than perfect, which means you don't know Him at all. And above all, He wants you to know Him.

Knowing God. I am sometimes overwhelmed at the task of wrapping my consciousness around just what that means. He is I AM, the One in whom and by whom all things are. He is holy. Every aspect of His being is infused by and enveloped in His holiness. His righteousness is a holy righteousness. His power is a perfectly holy power. He's more perfect than "perfect" knows how to be. As pure as "pure" is, it is less pure than God. He is justice and truth; He is merciful, all-knowing, ever present, and unchanging from everlasting to everlasting. And before I know it, my ponderings and ruminations have led me onto ground that never ceases to trouble me. Paul called it his wretchedness. David asked, *"What is man, that thou art mindful of him?"* (Psalm 8:4). They are more eloquent than I.

I remember the man I used to be. I know the man I still am. It seems almost cruel to me that God would give me a mind to understand how unworthy I am to receive any understanding of Him, much less *from* Him. And it seems crueler still to look at all that I have and to know what it cost Him to give it to me. I would not do the same for Him. I would not sacrifice my only son for Him. He knows that. My love for Him is not that great.

You cannot consider who God is for too long without being reminded of who you *aren't.* In those times God has seemed so far from me, so untouchable, so remote. Like David, I wonder why He bothers with me. It is at this point that my intellect fails me. It is also at this point that I believe God is at His most magnificent. In His Word, He shows me His eyes, able to see me no matter where I am. I find powerful arms, capable of snatching me from the jaws of every devouring enemy. I see a smile that makes all grace abound toward me, fingers that knitted me together in my mother's womb, and hands that daily guide and direct me through dangers seen and unseen. His ears hear my cries. He inhales the savor of my sacrifices, and His exhalation incinerates those who kindle His anger by their persecution of me. He loves me with a heart whose desire is toward me, and His insides ache when I am far from Him. Herein lies God's motive for making Himself known to us anatomically. It is to invite us to know Him intimately, to see Him as ultimately approachable, reachable, touchable, and accessible.

It is accurate to say that God's ways and thoughts are far above ours. It is also true that the breadth of Him extends beyond the capacity of the universe to contain it. He knows everything about everything. He is singularly powerful, awesome, and glorious. Only God could establish His throne. There was no one to appoint Him to His position, and certainly there is no one "God enough" to take it from Him. And yes, He is perfect in all His ways. But if we limit our view of God to those things that make Him heightless, groundless, bottomless, and boundless, then we have placed Him where He least wants to be: beyond our grasp.

*"Am I a God at hand, saith the LORD, and not a God afar off? Can any hide himself in secret places that I shall not see him? saith the LORD. Do not I fill heaven and earth? saith the LORD"* (Jeremiah 23:23–24). All creation was made to show man how great God is, so that he would fear Him and worship Him. But man was created to show God at His most caring and intimate. We were made in His image, and He is love. We are,

therefore, pictures of God's love. To see Him anthropomorphically is to see Him in terms of His love for us. In this context, even our unworthiness bears witness, for God's mercy and grace take center stage when we realize how undeserving we are of His love.

God uses us to tell us that He is as close to us as He is far from us. We need to understand that fact if our picture of God is going to be complete. Infinitude without intimacy is the unkindest portrait we can paint of God. It is that of a child grabbing for an object that is being kept out of reach by a taller and stronger adult. The longer the game goes on, the more frustrated the child gets. He'll eventually give up. We will, too, if we limit our understanding of God to those aspects of His nature that keep Him "away" from us.

> Infinitude without intimacy is the unkindest portrait we can paint of God.

As we examine the anatomy of God in Scripture and see how men, women, and entire nations had their lives influenced and shaped by their understanding of it, a cycle begins to emerge. Our imaginations cannot contain the fullness of God any more than the universe can. So God progressively discloses Himself to His people while progressively creating within us an increasing capacity to comprehend each new disclosure. He stretches our sanctified imaginations just enough to hold a little bit more of Him. Then, once we get comfortable with that, He stretches them a little bit more.

This progression cannot take place without our consent or our active involvement, which makes sense because the goal of it is to bring us closer to God. At every stage, we are required to respond to God by making a choice that will signal our desire to continue on with Him. And as with all divine colaboring efforts, our participation is subject to and limited by the presence of sin in our lives. Sin separates us from God, and that separation prevents us from seeing Him, communicating with Him, coming to Him, and being changed by Him.

Sin, if it is allowed to build up in our lives, will gum up the workings of every spiritual pursuit. Prayer is hindered by sin. Gifts operate without power in sin. Wisdom becomes carnal and devilish in sin. Character is destroyed by sin, and honorable efforts are thwarted by it. Vision is obscured, ministry becomes powerlessness, and the path to God is obliterated by the darkness of sin.

We don't have the time or the space to go into detail about the crippling effects of sin. That's another book for another time. But I will say here that every believer should be in the habit of allowing the Holy Spirit to do a periodic sin check. Like David, we should cry, *"Search me, O God, and know my heart: try me, and know my thoughts: and see if there be any wicked way in me"* (Psalm 139:23–24). David was a man after God's heart not because he was the picture of sinless perfection, but because he was always willing to see sin as God saw it and was always willing to respond to it the way God responded to it. He exposed himself to the light of God's statutes, and if he found himself lacking, he moved immediately to confess and repent. David's life was marked by his relentless pursuit of God. *"One thing have I desired of the LORD, that will I seek after; that I may dwell in the house of the LORD all the days of my life, to behold the beauty of the LORD, and to inquire in his temple"* (Psalm 27:4). Everything David ever wanted was wrapped up, tied up, and tangled up in his longing to be in the presence of God. So, too, should all our aspirations be shaped and colored by a desire to see God and an unwillingness to accommodate the presence of sin.

When we submit ourselves to God's way, His will becomes clear to us. His desire to be known by us becomes obvious, and, more important, the cycle of working that desire out is put into operation.

## Revelation

Revelation exposes a part of God's anatomy to our view. It is that sovereign act of God that uncovers something previously hidden from us. As I mentioned before, God can't bare Himself to us all at once. We couldn't handle it. The consuming fire of His holiness would destroy our humanity. So God mercifully unveils Himself to us a bit at a time according to three criteria: (1) our desire to see, (2) our ability to see, and (3) our need to see.

God does not reveal Himself to the son or daughter who doesn't want to see Him. Throughout Scripture, we are told to seek God, set our affections on Him, run after Him, grope for Him, call out to Him, and incline or lean toward Him. All those activities require effort on our part, but more important, they are always preceded by a preference or tendency toward God. God never forces Himself on us. Love is always a choice. He chose us, and He is willing to risk not being chosen by us in order to allow us to experience the divine nature of His love in its fullness.

Once it is established that we want to see God, the next part of revelation considers our qualifications for receiving it. As I mentioned before, sin disqualifies us as recipients of the things of God. Another thing that disqualifies us is our refusal to act on the last revelation He gave us. God is not wasteful. He doesn't move on to a new lesson until the old one is learned. He won't give new revelation where the current one withers in our fear or unbelief. Every revelation of God tells us something about God and prepares us for the next revelation. If we refuse to receive Him, we diminish our ability to receive more of Him.

Last, all revelation is given from God on a need-to-know basis. If you need to know that God hears your cries, then He will reveal His listening ears to you at just the right time. If you need to know that His hand will provide for you in the wilderness, I promise, you will see it. If you need to see God's eyes, He will not show you His mouth. Now, there's a flip side to this. You may think that what you need to see in your crisis is provision from the hand of God. But what God may want to show you is the peace that comes from the awareness that His ears hear your cries. It is God who addresses your need, and, my friend, it is also God who determines what your need is. Every revelation will be according to His purpose, and that purpose was established even before your need was.

In revelation, we know that God is. Hebrews 11:6 says that before we come to Him, we must first believe that He is. Our response to the revelation of God, therefore, is simply to see what He shows us; it is to accept that in that moment, something has been uncovered and placed before our spirits for perusal.

## Recognition

Once our spirits have beheld a particular aspect of God, our minds have to make the proper attributions concerning it. Recognition places every revelation in a spiritual archive of understanding. Where revelation says, "I see something," recognition acknowledges that "I see *God.*" It's at this point that every believer has to accept or reject responsibility for what he now knows.

I've been to board meetings where men and women raised their hands and cleared their throats in an attempt to make it obvious to the person conducting the meeting that they wanted to be seen and ultimately heard. But until the chairman "recognized" them, they could not speak. God makes it obvious to you that He wants to be recognized. Recognizing Him involves a twofold act of directing your attention to Him, then communicating your willingness to hear Him. Now keep in mind that recognition, like anything else with God, is for your benefit, not God's. He's no more important because you recognize Him. Rather, recognition is your acknowledgment that He is more important *to you.*

Have you ever seen somebody coming toward you in the distance, and you decided to walk on the other side of the street because you didn't want to deal with that person at that moment? Well, the fact that you never had to engage in conversation with him doesn't negate the fact that you did see him. We try to play that same game with God. We see Him, but we think that if we don't acknowledge Him, we absolve ourselves of the responsibility of responding to Him. Let me tell you a little secret. God saw you coming before you saw Him, and there is no path wide enough for you to avoid Him.

The same spirit that allows us to recognize God also shows us when something or someone is not God. Not every dollar offered to help you out of a jam comes from the coffers of God. Sometimes the enemy's hand looks a lot like God's if we're not using our spiritual eyes. Recognition, then, is affected and sometimes distorted by the condition of our hearts. A heart fueled by fear, bitterness, anger, unforgiveness, or pride will weaken a person's recognition capabilities. A woman, for example, who harbors a fear of being alone may recognize an unsanctified, unsanctioned love affair as "God-ordained." I also have seen people unable to hear godly counsel through their anger.

It's obvious, then, that recognition always has to be run through the filter of the Word of God. In order to recognize God in someone or in the midst of some situation, we have to be able to place it next to what God has already said in His Word. If it doesn't line up, then we have to consider what we see as a revelation of other than divine origins.

Our response in recognition is to move—to move toward whatever is acknowledged to be God and away from what is not of Him. Jesus said, *"Behold, I stand at the door, and knock: if any man hear my voice, and open the door..."* (Revelation 3:20). Notice that the door doesn't open until the person inside hears a voice. In fact, Jesus implied that the opening of the door is preceded by the person's understanding and acknowledging that Christ is definitely the One knocking at the door. He said, *"If any man hear **my** voice"* (emphasis added). Whenever God reveals Himself to us, He always allows us the opportunity to accept or ignore Him. By ignoring Him, we ask Him to stop talking, stop moving, and stop acting on our behalf. And He will back off until we say otherwise. But our acceptance, that is, our recognition of God, invites Him to add color, dimension, and depth to our relationship with Him.

## Relationship

> *And I say unto you, Ask, and it shall be given you; seek, and ye shall find; knock, and it shall be opened unto you. For every one that asketh receiveth; and he that seeketh findeth; and to him that knocketh it shall be opened.* (Luke 11:9–10)

Most of us have passed by these verses of Scripture in our studies, heard them preached from a pulpit or two, or caught them as they flew by on snatches of spiritual conversation. They comprise, I think, one of the more obvious illustrations of the reciprocity we enjoy in being in relationship with God. We ask, and it is given. We seek and then find. We knock, and the door is opened unto us. It is plain that we are not by ourselves, adequate within ourselves, or able to acquire what we need on our own. There are some things we need that we don't have, so we ask God for them. There are some things we have that are not sufficient, so we seek them out and God leads us. There are some areas of sufficiency that God wants to add to, so we inquire at the doors He places in front of us.

# The Anatomy of God

What makes this passage special to us as we consider God's desire to show Himself to us is found when we consider the grammatical tenses of the verbs *ask, seek,* and *knock*. They are expressed as present imperatives in verse 9 and as present participles in verse 10. Both tenses indicate continuous or repeated action. In other words, in this passage, Jesus was telling us to keep on asking, keep on seeking, keep on knocking, over and over. The implication is that you will keep on receiving, finding, and having doors opened to you in response. This is, in essence, what it means to experience relationship with God.

When the Lord reveals a part of Himself to us and we recognize His presence in our lives, it should lead every willing heart to examine every implication of that revelation. When I see, for example, the protective arm of God shielding me from hurt, harm, and danger and I acknowledge Him in my life as my strength and buckler, then I begin to understand how He kept me when I didn't know how to call on Him, when I didn't even know that was an option. I start to get a little braver about my tomorrows because I know that He will be watching over me. I see His mercy, grace, long-suffering, and love colored with His desire to protect me. As I study every facet and fold of this newly understood aspect of God, my prayers take on new depth and boldness. My praise is expanded, and my worship is more complete. The more I see of God, the more I want to know, so the more I ask, seek, and knock.

Relationship is the flowering of the curiosity created by every new unveiling of God's person to us. It is through relationship that intimacy knits us to the very heart of the Almighty. Most couples fall in love gradually as they learn about each other. As God teaches us more and more about Himself and reveals more and more of His heart to us, we fall more and more in love with Him, and we get an increasingly clearer understanding of how in love with us He already is. Remember, God already knows everything about us. In relationship with Him, He's telling us not only who He is, but also who we are.

An odd thing happens in relationship with God. As our intimacy with Him increases, a strange paradox arises within us. God appears to be more loving, while we appear to be less lovable. As He becomes more wonderful to us, we become more full of wonder that He not only loves us but also *chooses* to love us. At this point we can choose to be overwhelmed with shame, overinflated with pride, or overcome with gratitude. The first option will cause us to resist God. The second will cause God to resist us. But the third will transform us.

## Reflection

I can't say that I'm completely comfortable with knowing that I have crossed the divide between "young man" and, well, the guy I am now. What I find most unnerving about aging is that it doesn't happen with your permission or within your scope. Time takes its toll on you stealthily, prompting elastic musculature to pack its bags and whisper to quite a few of the hairs on your head, "The achy joints and the grays have arrived. Our work is done here." So youth creeps out of you, its departure muffled by the thunderous footfalls of Obligation and Responsibility, adulthood's tireless companions. Nobody leaves you so much as a Post-It Note. The mirror is the only one kind enough—or cruel enough—to break the news to you. As time continues to steal features and faculties from you, your reflection continues to report it. It doesn't lie to you, and it won't let anyone else lie to you. It keeps an accurate account of your relationship with time.

Spiritually speaking, our reflection keeps an accurate account of our relationship with God. Every encounter with God is documented in our reflection. How we appear spiritually tells others and us about how well we're getting along with Him. Over time, laughter, a healthy diet, smoking, exercise, stress, alcohol, and drugs will tell their story on the body of a person. Likewise, faith, fear, bitterness, joy, contentment, peace, pride, and anger will imprint the spirit, depending on our relationship with God.

Reflection is God's way of telling us that He is at work in us. It is confirmation that He has entered the door we opened and has consented to sup with us. In relationship, we come to know a person better. When we reflect a person, we have decided that he is worth emulating. God is perfect, which means we're not in relationship with Him for Him to become more like us. The goal is to become more like Him, so when we reflect Him, that is His signal to us that the relationship is working. Revelation says, "I see." Recognition says, "I see God." Relationship declares, "I see God with me." Reflection shouts, "I see God *in me*!"

Reflection is God's glory produced in us. And because God's glory is always greater than we are, any exposure to it and expression of it expands us and changes us. In other words, when we reflect God's glory, we see Him in ourselves. His reflection becomes a new revelation to us. The cycle of revelation, recognition, relationship, and reflection begins anew, on another level. As God becomes more visible *to* us, He is also becoming more visible *in* us. Then we live out the goal of the cycle, which is to participate in the divine nature even as we are transformed to express it. Paul called it being transformed *"from glory to glory"* in 2 Corinthians 3:18. In Psalm 84:7 man is said to go from *"strength to strength."* And in Romans 1:17, the righteousness of God is said to be unveiled *"from faith to faith."* Each of these phrases suggests progressive exposure to the things of God.

Not surprisingly, our own anatomy reveals this very pattern. You wouldn't give a newborn a fifty-pound dumbbell to lift. He couldn't handle the weight of it. He can barely raise his bottle to his mouth. But after he has grown some and gotten some muscles, some coordination, and some understanding, the baby-turned-young man will be able to lift that and eventually more. The more we grow, the more we're able to do. The same thing is true in our fellowship with God. It is a process.

## A Model of Perfection

As a pastor, I will have to stand before God one day and give an account of the men and women who have been left in my care. He will look at all my congregation and examine their hearts to see if the Word He entrusted to me found its way there, and if it has, He will check to see if it was watered and watched to the best of my ability. As a preacher and teacher, I can expect to be held responsible for studying to show myself approved before God and for communicating what I learned, not just in word, but also in deed, for Paul said that I am to be an example for those whom God has placed in my custody. (See 2 Thessalonians 3:9.)

That accounting will include more than just the membership of Faithful Central Bible Church in Los Angeles, California. It also will include those pastors who fall under my supervision as presiding bishop of the Macedonia International Bible Fellowship. It even will extend to the people who read my books and listen to my tapes, if I consider what Christ said to the Pharisees in Matthew 12:36–37: *"But I say unto you, That every idle word that men shall speak, they shall give an account thereof in the day of judgment. For by thy words thou shalt be justified, and by thy words thou shalt be condemned."* Although I know that was not an exhortation made specifically to pastors, I am considered among the men (and women) who have the potential to speak idly.

To be honest, there have been times when I have wished I could be absolved of my pastoral responsibilities, though not for the reasons you might think. I don't mind the things that some pastors consider to be the "headaches" of ministry. I enjoy the work that goes into preparing my sermons. Dealing with different personalities, especially in leadership, can be tedious, but it's not unbearable enough to make me question my call. I have seen senior pastors who never developed a love for people. I am not in that number. I am honored and humbled at the people I have been blessed to shepherd.

But as I preach, teach, lead, and watch over them, I walk a kind of spiritual tightrope. As a preacher, I want people to listen to me, but I want them to hear God. As a teacher, I want people to understand, but I want their understanding to go beyond what I've said to what God is saying to them. People should follow you if you're a leader. If you say you're a leader and nobody is following you, you're just taking a walk. But there's a thin line between *following* me and following *me*. I am called to watch over the people of God, but the people are not my possession. They are God's. I'm just a steward. I never want to stand before God one day and be accused of stealing God's property. I have at times wished I was not accountable for the people of God because of a very real danger present for any pastor who takes his call seriously. We run the risk of producing good clones instead of good Christians. It's too easy to fall into the trap of being satisfied as long as our congregation comes to church every Sunday, listens, shouts, dances, gives, then goes home without a complaint, without checking to see if they have a personal relationship with God—one that doesn't require us as a go-between. We can become so busy with carrying crippled people to God that we won't be able to do what we were called to do, and that is carry the healing Word of God to the crippled people. If we're not careful, we'll be judged for trying to create God in our own image instead of allowing God to recreate us in His.

Every once in awhile, I have to remind people that my arms may be able to hug them, but, unlike God's arms, they will fall short of saving. My eyes don't see everything. I may miss that deep pain in their hearts. And if I do see it, I can't make them whole again. From time to time I have to remind myself that I didn't climb up on a cross and die, so I can't keep some people out of hell, and I certainly can't be counted on to be sinless, sacrificial, or selfless all the time. I will not bat a thousand in those areas. I won't even come close. Mercy suits my case as much as anybody else's.

Because I'm not God, I will leave you. Because I'm not Christ, I will forsake you. I want you to hear what I'm saying because I know I'm not the only one who has tried to save the world. And I know I'm not the only one who has looked for salvation in things and people other than God.

I believe this book is, in part, God's word to all of us that He is, and will always be, our only Hero. My prayer is that it would reveal God to you in a way that will confront you, challenge you, and change you. As we focus on the anatomy of God, consider the loving-kindness that placed the miraculous image of almighty God not right next to you, but right *on* you and right *in* you. He did that so you'd know that He would never be further from you than you are from Him. He wants you to study Him, up close and personal. He wants to teach you what it means to live, move, and have your being in Him by living, moving, and being in you.

> This book is, in part, God's word to all of us that He is, and will always be, our only Hero.

You will find, as you seek to understand the anatomy of God, that whenever God shows you anything about His person, it always tells you something about His personality. God is in actuality a Spirit. His only reason for showing Himself to us anatomically is to help us get a handle on His nature. That's why what we're going to see of God's anatomy is as significant as what we won't see. We won't see, for example, the knees of God or the legs of God. Knees or kneeling in Scripture depict submission, fear, begging, or worship. None of these is a quality or behavior of God. All are behaviors of man toward God.

Legs appear in the Bible as an image of human strength. Psalm 147:10 says that God *"taketh not pleasure in the legs of a man,"* meaning He's not impressed with man's power. It is not surprising, then, that we don't find an actual reference to "the legs of God" in Scripture, despite instances where we read of people "walking" with God. Legs also move us from one place to another and figuratively represent our way of life, lived out day to day. God is eternally self-existent, living outside of time; His life doesn't unfold or "happen" the way ours do. He just *is.* Moreover, He doesn't move from one place to another. He is omnipresent, in all places at all times at the same time.

The shoulders represent labor or work. God ceased from His labors after six days, so we will not find the shoulders of God pictured in Scripture. The neck is used to reference servitude, submission, or complete subjection. God is God, and beside Him there is none other. He reigns supreme above all things always. The neck is also illustrative of the inward inclination of the heart. Israel was called a *"stiffnecked people"* (Exodus 32:9), an allusion to their hearts, which were resistant to the things of God. We will learn in a later chapter that the heart of God is revealed in all the other parts of His anatomy.

Presenting our back to another person means we are rejecting him, and because we serve a God who has said He would never leave or forsake us, we don't see Him showing us His back. Moses saw God's "back side" as He passed by, but that was to spare Moses certain death at facing His holiness head-on. Only Jesus has beheld God fully, according to John, who proclaimed in his Gospel that the Son exists *"in the bosom of the Father"* and has declared Him unto us (John 1:18). The Bible speaks of Israel's King Jeroboam casting God behind his back, and of Israel doing the same with His statutes; this is the ultimate rebuff. (See 1 Kings 14:9; Nehemiah 9:26; Ezekiel 23:35.) That is something we never see God doing—except when it comes to His forgiving our sins. (See Isaiah 38:17.)

We humans are prone to seeing all things from a very egocentric perspective. God knows this, or He would not make the effort to paint a picture of Himself on the canvas we spend the most time looking at—ourselves. One day we will all stand before Him to account for our time here, and the only question that will concern Him on that day will be, "Do you look like Me?" If we have been diligent to read the love letter He has penned to us on the parchment of our own fallible and fault-ridden frames, we will rejoice to answer Him. If we will stop wondering what God has to say on earth about us and start seeking out what we have to say on earth about Him, then our vanity will not have been in vain. If you finish this book and all you learn is that you were made for God's pleasure and not He for yours, you will have learned much. What an amazing thing it will be to know that you please God!

The gifts on this journey you are about to take are many and varied. As God reveals His spectacular body to you, you will discover the glory of His awesome love for you. You'll discover that He is not hiding from you. In fact, Acts 17:27 says we were made to come looking for Him: *"That they should seek the Lord, if haply they might feel after him, and find him, though he be not far from every one of us."*

Shall we?

# Two

# To See You Smile: The Face of God

> A kindergarten teacher told everyone to draw a picture of what
> was important to them. In the back of the room Johnny began
> to labor over his drawing. Everybody else finished and handed
> in their picture, but he didn't. He was still drawing. The teacher
> graciously walked back and put her arm around Johnny's shoul-
> der and said, "Johnny, what are you drawing?" He didn't look
> up; he just kept on working feverishly at his picture. He said,
> "God." "But Johnny," she said gently, "no one knows what God
> looks like." He answered, "They will when I'm through."
> —Em Griffin, *The Mind Changers*

I think my wife, Togetta, is one of the most beautiful women
I know. You might say I'm biased, and I admit I am. She
is my wife, and I love her dearly. Being biased, though,
doesn't make me blind. She really is fine. I've heard people
say that when you've been married for a lot of years, you stop
seeing your spouse with your eyes and start looking at him
or her with your heart. That's sweet, but praise God, after

twenty-five years, my eyes are still quite happy. In fact, I'm glad she's my wife because, if she were somebody else's wife, I'd get in a whole lot of trouble for looking at her the way I do.

She has a wonderful face. Like most husbands, I like it more when she's smiling, and I like it most when I'm the reason she's smiling. In a room crowded with people, I find myself looking for her for no reason other than just to see her face. No, I don't look longingly into her eyes. I don't hear a symphony and weave my way through a sea of bodies for the touch of her hand. I simply see her, and she sees me see her, and the moment passes. But, it has to be her face. It's not enough to see the back of her head or the outline of her frame. I'm not satisfied until her face comes into view.

There is something about a face that connects us to people in ways no other part of the anatomy can. Intimate partners and strangers alike depend on its expression and impression to initiate, enrich, and punctuate every kind of communication. The face is the first thing we look for and the first thing that looks for us. It is what we remember most about another person and what we believe first. If I tell you that I've missed you, my face can make that a lie. If I declare my heart is cut to the quick, my tortured visage can affirm and confirm that spoken pain.

The face, then, is the anatomy's chief instrument of self-expression. We are, for better or worse, our face. Usually our face will tell people how we are doing. A sad face means a sad person. This may seem elementary until you begin to consider the face of God. The face gives us our first impression of someone. What was your first impression of God? Did His face look like holiness? Was His expression omniscience or righteousness? Did you see peace when you caught a glimpse of Him? What did God's face tell you about how He was feeling? Was He happy? You don't know, do you?

*We are, for better or worse, our face.*

You cannot know, because God Himself said in Exodus that no man could see His face and live.

Why are there so many references, then, to the face of God in Scripture? And why does God tell us to *"seek his face"* (Psalm 105:4)? Obviously God wants to reveal something about Himself to us through our understanding of the expression, appearance, and operation of the face.

The movie *Shrek* was an amazing work in animation. The makers of the film took great pride in the effort that went into making the characters appear more "alive" than they ever had up to that point in the genre. It was interesting to find out that in the title character, animators working with computers had more than three hundred points of movement in the face alone. In other words, human faces are so complex in the way they move that in order for Shrek's face to appear as "human" as possible, the artists and engineers had to manipulate its movement in more than three hundred places. I couldn't point to three hundred places on my own face, but that gives you an idea of how complex a feature the face is.

With God it's no different. Everything that God is resides in His face, so to seek His face is to seek to see Him. Now since we can't actually see God, He must have had something else in mind when He told us to seek Him and promised that He would be found. I want to look at a number of passages in Scripture in an effort to illuminate this issue of the face of God. I will remind you here, and at various times throughout this book, that anthropomorphic references to God are for our benefit, so any examination of the revelation of God's anatomy has to include the response of man to that revelation. In other words, we don't seek to understand something about the face of God apart from God's expectations of us in that context.

> Everything that God is resides in His face.

# The Anatomy of God

The face of God is referred to throughout the Bible, but we're going to stay primarily in the Psalms, which present the most vivid personal images of man's search for God. The Psalms are our own emotions exposed and vulnerable before God and man. If we will let them, they will uncover every evil thing lurking in our hearts and challenge it with the truth of God's mercy and grace. I'm not always comfortable with the Psalms. They show me more than I want to see sometimes. However, they also spread before me a glorious portrait of the multifaceted nature of God, and an exquisite rendering of His face in particular.

## An Audience with Him

*The LORD is my light and my salvation; whom shall I fear? the LORD is the strength of my life; of whom shall I be afraid?...For in the time of trouble he shall hide me in his pavilion: in the secret of his tabernacle shall he hide me; he shall set me up upon a rock. And now shall mine head be lifted up above mine enemies round about me: therefore will I offer in his tabernacle sacrifices of joy; I will sing, yea, I will sing praises unto the LORD. Hear, O LORD, when I cry with my voice: have mercy also upon me, and answer me. When thou saidst, Seek ye my face; my heart said unto thee, Thy face, LORD, will I seek. Hide not thy face far from me; put not thy servant away in anger: thou hast been my help; leave me not, neither forsake me, O God of my salvation.* (Psalm 27:1, 5–9)

This is a psalm of David. He said, "Lord, when I call upon You, hear me and have mercy on me. Have mercy on me because when You said, 'Seek My face,' my heart said, 'Lord, Your face will I seek.'" God told the psalmist to seek His face. That in itself is a revelation of the will of God. He desires that you and I would be face seekers, people anxious to see the face of God.

Seeking the face of God has a number of connotations. First and most obvious is the image of seeking the audience of God. David called it inquiring of God in His temple. The temple of God is anywhere God's presence resides. Therefore, seeking God's presence is the picture of a person going over to God's house to hang out with Him.

In Psalm 27:7 David said that when he calls on God, he wants the Lord to have mercy upon him. When we seek to be with God, we automatically need mercy because, as I mentioned earlier, the Bible says no man will see the face of God and live. Jacob was stunned at having *"seen the face of God"* (Genesis 33:10) and not being struck dead. Of course, Jacob didn't see God's naked face. He couldn't handle that. The face of God, the essence of the glory of God, then, was filtered through His love and mercy; its full radiance was covered in a sheath of His kindness and grace. God's mercy is in effect 24 hours a day, 7 days a week, 52 weeks a year, because He wants us to seek His face.

To seek means to have a sincere desire for something. In this context it means one sincerely wants an audience with God. That's why, when God told the psalmist to seek Him, the response was, "My heart said, 'I will seek Your face.'" The seeking of God's face is not done with the eyes or other human senses. God doesn't want you to seek Him unless you want to. He's not looking for curious Christians. He doesn't have time for "lookie-loos." He's not into "drive-by" devotion, where you're just checking in to say hey and amen. The seekers whom God is seeking have a sincere desire in their hearts to find Him. Is your goal in life to live before the face of God? Then He wants you to seek Him.

Psalm 24 gives us some other requirements for seeking an audience with God. Psalm 24 is a part of a group of psalms called "Psalms of Ascent." These were songs designated to be sung when the people of God went up to the temple or came to Jerusalem to worship God. If you go to Israel today, you'll discover that there is a mountain there, and on it are the remains of the wall where the temple was originally. There are steps leading up to the wall, and those steps come up out of a valley. In order to come up to the temple, the worshippers would walk, sometimes by the thousands, from all over the then-known world, through the valley to the foot of the mountain. They always stopped at the foot of the mountain, where a ritual of praise would take place.

Here's the scene. The people are on their way to the temple. They are on their way to commune with God, to be with God, to seek His face. They come through the valley and stop at the base of the mountain, and a priest would say what we find in Psalm 24:3–4:

> *Who shall ascend into the hill of the LORD? or who shall stand in his holy place?*

It's sort of a "call and response" song because another priest would say the next verse:

> *He that hath clean hands, and a pure heart; who hath not lifted up his soul unto vanity, nor sworn deceitfully.*

They make that declaration, and then they would proceed up the steps into the temple and into the presence or the face of God, hence the designation "Psalms of Ascent."

What I want you to see here is another requirement for the believer who seeks the face of God. Who will ascend into the presence of God? Who will be allowed to see His face? It is he who has clean hands and a pure heart. Many of us at this point would just excuse ourselves to the priests and say, "Fellows, you all head up the stairs without me. I'll be waiting here when you get back." If the qualification is clean hands and a pure heart, you're thinking that's not your crowd.

However, *"clean hands, and a pure heart"* is not a declaration of righteousness. It is a declaration of a *desire* for righteousness. It was not the requirement per se to enter into the presence of God. It was the spoken desire for a *result* of being in God's presence. Verse 6 of the same psalm says that these are those who seek God's face. Those who desire to come into the presence of God come into His presence and therefore have their hands and hearts cleansed. It reveals God's standard and acknowledges God's standard. But it also speaks to the fact that I cannot meet God's standard in and of myself. I need God to produce that standard in me. I don't have clean hands and a pure heart, but I do seek His face. And as I seek His face and He allows me into His presence by His mercy, I get my hands clean and my heart purified. It's not a requirement. It is the result of being in His presence because it is a revelation of God's standard to me.

To see the face of God is to have an audience with Him so He can remind us of the call upon our lives. We are called to have clean hands and a pure heart, which suggests being righteous before God. Being righteous, or right, before God is always the combination of what's inside and what's outside. Clean hands outside; pure heart inside. It's not an either/or situation. You don't have an option. It's both/and.

Righteousness is a life of integrity and character—character before men and integrity before God. It's not only what I do internally, but it's also how I live my life externally according to God's standard. For many of us, the problem is that we set standards by watching people. Our concern, then, is not how clean our hands are, but only that they be cleaner than someone else's. And because all our hands are dirty, nobody gets clean. The only standard is the one set by God and revealed in the presence of God. Face it. It doesn't matter if I can jump only ten feet and you can jump twenty feet. If we're both jumping across the Grand Canyon, everybody is going to fall.

God wants you to be clean on the inside and on the outside. He's concerned not just with how you talk, but also with how you walk; not just with what you think, but also with what you do; not just what you believe, but how you behave; not just principles, but practice; not just what you know, but how you act because you know what you know. Clean hands and a pure heart.

By the way, God is not just thinking about your own personal hands and heart. Verse 6 of Psalm 24 makes that clear where the author wrote, *"This is the generation of them that seek him."* God is always concerned about more than just you; He's concerned about generations. He does not allow you into His presence to teach you, bless you, and change you just for you. He is concerned about your children, your grandchildren, and your great-grandchildren. He looks for generations who will seek Him.

We live in a society of people consumed with seeking itself. We live in bondage to materialism and secularism because we have not been taught to seek the things of God. We have not prioritized the things of God. But if we make God our priority and seek an audience with Him, He will show us how to live our lives for Him and then how to raise generations who will do the same.

### Knowing His Assistance

*Seek the LORD, and his strength: seek his face evermore.*
(Psalm 105:4)

Seeking the face of God is to have or know His assistance. Psalm 105 implies that there is a relationship between the face of God and the strength of God. His face is related to His help, His empowerment, and His aid. When we come into His presence, we understand that what He requires of us cannot be done in our own strength. I can't live the way God wants me to live by my own wisdom and understanding. In fact, one writer in Proverbs cautioned us not to live by our own understanding but by the assistance and guidance of the Lord. So I seek His face, and His face gives me a revelation of His strength.

Probably one of the best ways to understand the assistance of God or the strength of God, in a context of seeking the face of God, is to look at what happens when His face is not there. Psalm 27:8 finds the writer promising to seek God's face. The next verse says, *"Hide not thy face far from me."* So, then, the God who can reveal His face can hide it as well. I have good news and bad news for you on that front. The bad news is, God can hide His face from you. The good news is, God can hide His face from you. That sounds a little schizophrenic, I know. And we as humans can get that way when it comes to this idea of the face of God. We're not always quite sure if we want to see it or not. We do this crazy flip-flop with God sometimes. We flip out when He gets too far into our business, our marriage, our finances, and our relationships. If He shines too much light on us, He becomes the unwelcome guest. Then when we flop out there in the world all by ourselves, we want Him to come near.

Look at Psalm 51. King David had sinned before God. This is his psalm of repentance. Look especially at verse 9:

> *Hide thy face from my sins, and blot out all mine iniquities.*

This is the same David whose heart told God he would seek Him in Psalm 27. Here he was asking God to hide His face. I know how he felt. Have you ever done anything or saw something in yourself that you looked at and wanted to say, "Lord, don't look at that"? Have you ever had some stuff going on that you wanted to hide and cover up because you didn't want God to see it? Have you ever tried to sweep something under the carpet while you were praying? You figure if you don't mention it, God won't know about it, or maybe He'll just let it slide.

Earlier in Psalm 51, David said his sin was right in front of him. But he was asking God not to look at it. The sin was right in front of David's face, but he wanted God to turn His face from it. Did you get that? If something is in your face and you ask God not to look at it, you are, in essence, asking God not to look at you. Don't be too quick to ask God not to look at something. You might be asking Him to turn His face from you.

David said he would seek God's face in Psalm 27. In Psalm 51 he was saying, "Don't look. Hide Your face." Now look at Psalm 30.

> *I will extol thee, O Lord; for thou hast lifted me up, and hast not made my foes to rejoice over me. O Lord my God, I cried unto thee, and thou hast healed me. O Lord, thou hast brought up my soul from the grave: thou hast kept me alive, that I should not go down to the pit. Sing unto the Lord, O ye saints of his, and give thanks at the remembrance of his holiness. For his anger endureth but a moment; in his favour is life: weeping may endure for a night, but joy cometh in the morning.* (vv. 1–5)

David was giving testimony here. All is well. Now read the next verse:

> *And in my prosperity I said, I shall never be moved.*
> (v. 6)

Translation: "After You blessed me, I said, 'I can handle it from here.'" David was dancing and singing and praising the Lord for hearing his cry, delivering him, healing him, getting him out of a pit, making his enemies leave him alone, helping him through his dark nights of weeping. Then, in his prosperity, he decided that things were okay. God could clock out now, take a break, and go on back up to heaven. "Good job, God. I'll call You back if I need You." Next verse:

*Thou didst hide thy face, and I was troubled.* (v. 7)

After his success, David got grand. After his blessing, after his healing, after his rescue, David decided he could handle things by himself. He could take on the mountains by himself. The Lord had set him up. As soon as he said, "I shall not be moved," God moved. He hid His face from David, and David was troubled.

There's a great dramatic Hebrew picture word for "trouble." It means to be in a tight place. When God hides His face, He hides His assistance and His strength. And that puts you in a tight place. That puts you in a jam. You can't turn and run because you can't turn in a tight place. Sometimes your place can get so tight that you can't even put your arms up. All you can do is holler, "Hey, Lord, look this way, please!"

You never want God to hide His face from you. Yes, it's rough to face Him sometimes. When He faces your sin, He has to deal with it—and with you. But if He ever turns His face from you, you're stuck with your sin and no God. How about that?

When God turns His face away, He's doing more than not looking in your direction. He's ignoring you. He has broken off communication with you. He has withdrawn His favor. When you call Him, He acts as though He can't hear you. Your prayers hit the ceiling and go no higher. Have you ever been in a situation in which you felt like you couldn't even get in touch with God? I know most of you reading this are real spiritual and this question doesn't apply to you. But some of us have been in some tight places with God. Some of us have made some wrong turns, blown it, followed the wrong person, went down the wrong path, and gotten so far away from God that we couldn't even call on Him. All we could do was hope that God mercifully looked our way because we realized that when He hid His face from us, we were in big trouble. On the other hand, some of us need for God to hide His face from us. Otherwise we'd keep living and running things on our own, never knowing we were in danger. For some of us, God needed to hide His face so we'd wake up.

Psalm 27, "I will seek Your face." Psalm 51, "Lord, don't look this way. Hide Your face." Psalm 30, "When You hid Your face, I was troubled." Now go to Psalm 69:17:

> *And hide not thy face from thy servant; for I am in trouble: hear me speedily.*

If I were God, I'd say, "Make up your mind! What do you want Me to do already?!" I love this verse. "Please, Lord, don't hide Your face from Your servant"—oh, now he's a servant. Isn't it funny how God humbles us? We get real grand sometimes. Then, when we get in a mess, we get so humble. "Hello? Lord? Begging Your pardon, Almighty. It's Your lowly servant, Father. Do You remember me? Please don't hide Your face from me."

I love the Word of God. Listen to the sequence. "I will seek Your face, Lord." "Lord, hide Your face." "When You hid Your face, I was in trouble." "Lord, please don't hide Your face. I'm in trouble over here!"

You're in trouble when God hides His face. You're in trouble when He withdraws His covering, lifts His favor, and backs off. Does He forsake you? No, His turning away is a response to your forsaking Him.

## Having His Acceptance

> *And the LORD spake unto Moses, saying, Speak unto Aaron and unto his sons, saying, On this wise ye shall*

*bless the children of Israel, saying unto them, The LORD bless thee, and keep thee: the LORD make his face shine upon thee, and be gracious unto thee: the LORD lift up his countenance upon thee, and give thee peace.*
(Numbers 6:22–26)

What does it mean to seek the face of God? It means to seek an audience with Him. It means knowing His assistance and strength. It also means to be accepted by God.

"May the Lord make His face to shine upon you." That speaks of the favor of God. When His face shines on your business, it means that business has the favor of God on it. When God makes His face to shine on your home, your family is covered by favor. Notice that God makes His face shine. It is an act of His will that is preceded by a desire in His heart. When you desire to seek His face, it is a choice your heart makes. Likewise, God chooses to make His face shine upon you. He chooses to flash His light in your direction.

"Shine" literally speaks of the shining of the sun. So this blessing God gave to Moses for His children says, "May God's mercy and favor radiate in your life." It is a declaration of a desire for you to know that you are accepted in the face of God and that that acceptance would be visible. To say that the face of God will shine and to liken His face to the shining of the sun is to suggest that God's face is always shining. It's not as though He starts shining and stops shining, then starts again. No. It's the sun. The sun never goes out. It's always shining somewhere.

Verse 26 adds to the blessing by pronouncing, "[May] *the LORD lift up his countenance upon thee.*" This is likened to the rising of the sun. Why is that significant? First of all, the idea of the sun rising implies that while it is always shining, you don't always see it. We will go through seasons when we cannot see the glow on the face of God, not because God is angry with us, but because there are times when we just can't see Him.

If you were reading this book by natural light, sooner or later it would be dark where you are, but not because the sun stopped shining. It'll just be shining in a different hemisphere of the world. Sometimes in your spiritual walk it will get dark, but it's not because God has turned His face from you. It doesn't matter how big your Bible is or how sweetly you sing in church. It won't matter how pretty your prayers are, how long you've been saved, or how well you speak in tongues. And you can quote Scriptures until Jesus comes back, but it will still get dark...because it's nighttime. And when it's nighttime, it's dark.

Nighttime is not always comfortable, but it is necessary. Nighttime is that time in your spiritual walk when everything you know to be true about God is put to the test. You will be tried and stretched during your nighttime. You will weep, as David did. You will not see the face of God, but you will have to trust that He has not left you or forsaken you. But don't lose heart, for as surely as nighttime comes, eventually it goes. Since the world was made, morning has followed evening. You just have to wait on it.

If you'll just wait through the night, sooner or later the sun will rise, no matter how dark the night was. It does not matter how strong the storm is, if you can just hold on through the night. It does not matter how dreary it is; it doesn't matter how bad things look. Just hold on. Alone or in a crowd, hold on. Your night might be a little longer than somebody else's—you might be trying to get through one of those Alaska nights that seem to go on forever—but if you can, just trust the faithfulness of the sun. Has it ever failed to rise on schedule?

When God does shine His face on your life, some folks will ask the wrong question. They'll ask you what God looked like when you saw His face. That's not the right question. The question is not what did God look like when you saw Him. The question is what did you look like after you saw Him? You see, Moses went to the top of Mount Sinai and saw the face of God, which, as I said, was not the raw, unshielded glory of God, but His glory draped and covered by the fragrance of His love. When Moses came down from that mountain, the Bible says his face was shining. Did you get that? When God shines on you, He makes you shine.

> The question is what did you look like after you saw Him?

Have you ever hugged somebody close enough for her makeup to rub off on you? One day my wife kissed me, and, shortly after that, I entered a room where some other people were. A couple of them saw her lipstick and figured they'd do me a favor and wipe it off. I wouldn't let them. I remember that I did not want that kiss wiped off because it brought back memories of a pleasant experience. I wanted the memory to last as long as possible.

When you come into the presence of the living God and He smiles on you, some of His shine rubs off on you, and even after you've gone about the rest of your business, you'll keep on shining. You may have come into His presence without a dime in your pocket, but you shine, child of God. You're struggling and being stretched, but you're still shining. You may be all by yourself in your situation, but you keep shining.

When God lifts up His countenance upon you, it means He's smiling. I want to make God smile. I want to live my life in such a way that when He looks into my life, He smiles. His smile indicates His pleasure and His acceptance. His smile. Have you ever considered just how much is communicated by a smile? Parents who are really wired to their children don't have to use a lot of words. Sometimes a parent at the bedside of a suffering child will muster up all the strength he or she has to smile and let that baby know that everything will be all right. There's something about mommy's or daddy's smile that chases fear away. There's something about the smile you get from your children. There's something about my wife's smile.

May the Lord bless you and keep you. May He make His face to shine upon you and be gracious unto you.

I pray that you would see His smile.

Three

# He Watches Me:
# The Eyes of God

When I panic, I run.
When I run, I lose.
When I lose, God waits.
When I wait, He fights.
When He fights, I learn.
—Charles Swindoll, *The Tale of the Tardy Oxcart*

The world changed during the writing of this book. On September 11, 2001, a blade of terrorism maliciously sliced through the seemingly flawless features of America's composure. So much has been written and said about the thousands who are dead, the millions still mourning, a once stable economy that now teeters as much as it totters, and the heroes—so many heroes—mined, refined, and defined by this still resonating calamity. My inclination was to leave any commentary on this to the pundits, politicians, priests, and preachers who can explain and expound with confidence and clarion wisdom to "Why?" and "What now?" and "Where do we go from here?" I am not in that number. I don't have a lot of answers. I must admit, my temptation was to withhold the meager offerings of my remarks and interpretations, and I would have but for the one question that has plagued me since that day.

God, did You see that?

I don't want to know anything else. I don't have to know why those children had to lose their parents. It grieves me, but I don't have to know why. I don't need to know where we go from this point. To be honest, I'm having a hard enough time trying to deal with today. Somebody opened an envelope yesterday, and today he's dead. Today there was another terrorist threat. Today twenty thousand men and women lost their jobs. Today is consuming me. Tomorrow is too much for me to think about right now. But I have to know, for my sanity, for my peace of mind, "Lord, did You see that? Did You *see* it?"

I grapple with that question. I wrestle with it and struggle with it, and soon I realize that I'm not the only one holding on in this fight. The question has gripped me as tightly as I have gripped it. Oh, my God. Yes, Lord. Thank You, Lord.

You have been waiting for us to ask this question. You have been waiting for us to open our mouths and ask what might make us seem a little less than holy. You have been waiting for us to ask the obvious, the question only a child would ask.

God, did You see that?

The eyes of God are a foregone conclusion for the believer. Of course God has eyes. He had to be able to see to create the world and run the universe. But what does it mean to say that? Blind people have eyes. People who wear glasses have eyes. Someone who avoids you has eyes. Someone who ignores you has eyes. People who are sleeping have eyes. People who don't know you and have formed negative opinions about you have eyes. The people who don't love you have eyes. What does it mean to say that God has eyes? It doesn't mean anything if He hasn't seen you.

When we consider this issue of the eyes of God, I want you to understand that His eyes are Spirit as He is. God sees spiritually. Our eyes take in light, shape, and depth in various forms, and we process those in our brains. Our brains then tell us what we're looking at, and it is at that point that we "see." God's eyes see, period. They look, process, and know all at the same time. God doesn't have to think about what He sees. He doesn't have to turn it upside down and inside out to get a thorough understanding of it. He knows everything about it at the exact moment that He sees it.

I don't have time to go into a deep theological discussion about how God, who lives outside of time, already saw what He sees before the beginning of the world began. That would blow your mind, and the purpose of this book is to deal with the God who chooses to reveal Himself within the confines of human intellect and understanding. So we're going to look at the eyes of God within the paradigm of the mechanics of human vision.

Because God looks, processes, and understands at the moment He sees, when we talk about the eyes of God, we are in fact talking about His omniscience. God doesn't just see the physical properties of something He's looking at; He sees the intellectual, spiritual, and social properties as well. He also knows how what He is looking at relates to the world it is in and the people around it, as well as how it will impact and be impacted by all things and all people in the future. All that and more are involved in God's visual faculties.

When we talk about the eyes of God, we are in fact talking about His omniscience.

I want to use three broad categories to deal with the eyes of God. I want to examine how He sees us, how He looks at us, and how He looks for us, in that order. That may seem backward since, after all, we look for something first, then look at it, and then see it. But with God, there is comfort in knowing that He sees us, responsibility in knowing that He is looking at us, and security in knowing that He is looking for us. Maybe it's just me, but I'd rather have the comfort of His closeness and then work my way out to feeling secure when He seems far away. Maybe that's not you, but I need that right now. I need to know that He sees me.

### Eyes That See Me

> In the LORD put I my trust: how say ye to my soul, Flee as a bird to your mountain? For, lo, the wicked bend their bow, they make ready their arrow upon the string, that they may privily shoot at the upright in heart.... The LORD is in his holy temple, the LORD's throne is in heaven: his eyes behold, his eyelids try, the children of men. (Psalm 11:1–2, 4)

The God who sees is all-knowing because the eyes of God see all and therefore know all things. Oftentimes in Scripture there is a reference to idol gods or those who worship idol gods, and one of the observations that is made repeatedly is that these idol gods, these handmade statues, have eyes but cannot see. Man makes his own little deity and puts eyes on it, but Scripture says the eyes cannot see. When man makes an idol, it is his attempt to make God in his own image. To say that the idol can't see is an amplification of that truth since only a man who is blind to the presence of God would craft an idol and hold it up before God.

David, however, declared the truth about the almighty and eternal God he served, saying that we serve and worship a God who doesn't just have eyes, but whose eyes see. This particular psalm is a vivid illustration of the operation of the eyes of God and how they see.

First of all, the psalmist showed us that God can see us in the context of a trial. The wicked were getting ready to shoot at him. The *New King James Version* uses the word *secretly* where it says *"privily."* Another version says *"in darkness."* The idea is that there is a climate of fear, frustration, and hopelessness. The situation was a grave one for David, the conquering king of Israel. He was, many scholars believe, on the run when this text was written. Some believe he was running from Saul, who was out to kill him and destroy him. Others think this psalm was penned in that season or period of time when he was running from his own son Absalom. Whatever the case, it is clear that David was under attack. He was going through something he identified as the enemy aiming bows and arrows at him and attacking him in darkness.

David was afraid. He wasn't paranoid. This was a real situation. There were people who wanted to see him dead. It can be argued here that the mention of bows and arrows is significant in this context because they can be construed to be weapons of a coward, since you can shoot at your target or your adversary without actually coming face to face with him. There's some support for this in the text since the enemy mentioned was trying to wage his battle *"secretly"* or *"in darkness."*

Let's look at this, then. David was being attacked by an enemy he couldn't see and being shot at with arrows he couldn't see. He was in the dark, the enemy was in the dark, and the arrows were in the dark. Have you ever been under attack like that? It's bad enough to have an enemy, but darkness throws a few other factors into the mix. Darkness means you don't know who the enemy is, what they look like, how close they are, and whether or not they are moving around you. Darkness cloaks the direction of the arrows and their size. You know you're in a stressful, dangerous situation. You want to defend yourself, but you can't see what you need to defend yourself from.

Second, David painted the picture of a God who can see you in your temptation. The temptation identified in the passage is very subtle, but it is unmistakable. The enemy was attacking him in the darkness, and out of that darkness a voice spoke and said, *"Flee as a bird to your mountain."* In the midst of a trial is where temptation will most likely raise its head. The voice told David to run. "Get out of here. There's no way out of this. You can't defeat this enemy. Run."

The trial created a climate of fear. This temptation speaks to the uncertainty that comes in a trial. David said, "You say to me...." Who is "you"? There are several options. "You" could be the enemy. The one who wants to destroy you is telling you to run to the mountains. The problem with that scenario is this: in battle, particularly in that part of the country David was from, the enemy often lurked in the mountains. It would be to the enemy's advantage, then, to have you run somewhere away from familiarity and into his grip.

Have you ever been faced with a dilemma and realized that if you make one mistake, your bad situation will be made worse? If it is the enemy tempting you to run in your trial, you can be sure his plan is to turn you away from God and into his hands.

"You" could have been God. There are legitimate times when God tells you to run. It would not be out of His character to instruct you to do this, not so much because you can't handle a situation as because your deliverance might be in another place. If you stay where you are, you may miss a blessing. It may not be God's plan for you to stay where you are. When God tells you to run, it may be to keep you from falling into some sin you might be helpless against. You do remember Joseph, don't you?

When sister Potiphar laid her dirty, filthy hands on Joseph, the Bible says Joseph took off. Call him a chicken, but the brother ran. In fact, he ran so fast that he left his clothes in the woman's hands. Sometimes it's better to be naked and embarrassed before man than to be fully clothed and ashamed before God.

Another possibility is that "you" could be your well-meaning friends. Sometimes people who genuinely care about us observe our situation and determine—often without checking with God—that we can't handle it and that it just makes good sense to run. Unfortunately, good sense isn't always God sense. They may have decided that you need to run because they were in the same situation once and they ran. Or they imagine that they would run if the circumstances were theirs. But we do not live by the wisdom of men. James said that man's wisdom can be carnal and devilish at times.

Finally, "you" could simply be you. David could have been talking to David. Have you ever tried to talk yourself out of staying in a bad situation, explaining to yourself that you shouldn't have to go through the pain of it or endure the hardship of it? Have you ever sat down and carefully created a handwritten, monogrammed, laced, cotton paper, personally engraved invitation to your own private pity party? You invited yourself. You were the guest of honor. You danced with yourself, talked to yourself, and told yourself how bad things were, and then you told yourself you shouldn't have to take that. Outraged, you told yourself, "You need to leave that mess. You ought to run." And you agreed with yourself.

Sometimes we tell ourselves that holiness is too high a price to pay. It's too lonely being chaste. We ought to run. Sometimes that voice tells us that the boss won't notice if a few things are missing. In other words, we ought to run from our integrity. Has a voice ever told you to run from the loneliness of being the only Christian where you work?

God sees us in our trials. He also sees us in our temptations. But how do we know that? David said it was dark.

How do we know God can see in the dark? Look at Psalm 139:11–12:

> If I say, Surely the darkness shall cover me; even the night shall be light about me. Yea, the darkness hideth not from thee; but the night shineth as the day: the darkness and the light are both alike to thee.

I love it. There are two things I want you to see here. First and most obvious is that darkness and light don't make any difference to God, who sees with His Spirit. Your enemies can hide from you in the dark, but they can't hide from God. The second thing is that the night becomes light around you. Wait a minute. How does night become light? What turns the lights on in the night seasons of your life? Faith is the divine switch of every believer. Faith comes by hearing and hearing by the Word of God (Romans 10:17). When you're in the dark, the only thing you have to depend on is what God has already said to you. If He said He would never leave you or forsake you, then He must be with you in the dark. If He said no weapon formed against you will prosper, then those arrows in the dark may hit you, but they won't kill you. If He said resist the enemy and he will flee, you stand there in the dark and call the devil a liar.

The Word of God is a *"lamp unto* [your] *feet and a light unto* [your] *path"* (Psalm 119:105). The Word lights your way in the darkness, but it's very interesting how it works. It doesn't make all things visible to you; it just tells you where everything is. When you're in your darkness, you may not be able to see the enemy, but the Word will give you his coordinates so that you'll know his position in relation to you. Still don't get it? Let me see if I can make this clearer.

Bats can't see. But, if you put them in a room full of furniture, they can fly around all day and never hit anything. That's because they have an unusually keen sense of hearing. Sound waves bounce off everything, and they know by hearing how far away something is, how it's shaped, and what its density is. Likewise, the Spirit of Truth that lives in you—and the Truth is the Word—will bring to your remembrance everything you need to know to make it in the darkness. You may want to give up, but the Word of God says, *"Let patience have her perfect work"* (James 1:4). You may want to panic, but the Word says, "Worry for nothing." (See Philippians 4:6.) You may think that you're alone, but the Word says, "Nothing shall separate you from the love of God." (See Romans 8:39.) The Word will let you know if you're in the gutter because of your own sin, or if you're in your Gethsemane, the place where God stretches you just before you walk into your destiny. The Word makes all things visible to your spirit, if you believe it. Without faith, the Word is just a bunch of words on a page.

The key to handling the trial and the temptation is not to know just that God sees the trial and the temptation, but to know the *God* who is looking at them. That's because God is not even looking at the trial or the temptation. He's looking at you. And what He wants to see is your trust. If He can see that, He will move mountains for you. The eyes of God, which see everything, can see whether or not you trust Him.

David said in Psalm 11:1, *"In the LORD put I my trust."* These are the very first words of the psalm. That's not an accident. Before the trial, before the darkness, before the arrows, before the temptation to run, David put his trust in the Lord. The trust happened, and then he went on to tell how he was being attacked by the enemy. It's like he was trying to make sense of it. He couldn't quite explain it. And in his confusion, he was hearing a voice telling him to run and throw in the towel.

Does this sequence sound familiar? You put your trust in God, and then the attack comes. You weren't doing so badly out there in the world. Then you decided to put your trust in

God. All was wonderful and spiritual and exciting…but then the darkness seemed to come out of nowhere. But you had already put your trust in the Lord. It seemed like as soon as you determined that you would live holy, all hell broke loose. You know what? That's exactly what happened.

You didn't think satan was going to give you up without a fight, did you? You didn't think he was going to just sit by and watch you ravage the gates to his kingdom through the power of your ministry, did you? I know you don't think he won't try to take you out every chance he gets. But he should have attacked you before God saw your trust.

Think about that. The God who sees your trust saw that before He saw you in the darkness. I'll tell you a little secret. He allowed the darkness to happen so that you'd see what He sees: a person who trusts Him enough to listen for His voice in the darkness; a person who knows how to get to peace in darkness; a person who knows that perfect love casts out fear in the darkness. *"Flee as a bird?"* (Psalm 11:1). The devil doesn't even know how much God loves you! Jesus said you're worth more to God than a bird. And God is so much more a refuge than a mountain. The eyes of God see me. They see my trials, and they see my temptation. But first, they see my trust.

Psalm 11:4 says that God's eyes *"behold."* The tense of the verb makes it more accurately rendered, "His eyes are beholding." He is seeing. He continues to see, and He is continually seeing. His eyes are continually seeing into my life. It means that God is not just taking a passing glance at me; He gazes at me. The word literally means "to cut, dissect, or split." God cuts through all the stuff in my life, and His gaze zeroes in on me.

The eyelids of God come into play here. It says in our passage that the eyelids of God *"try"* men (v. 4). It's a great picture of a person squinting to see something clearer. God squints to check out the intimate details of my life. His squinting goes into the smallest, darkest, most recessed place in my heart and exposes the things in me that even I don't know about. You may wonder at this point why a God who can see everything would even need to squint.

God's squinting His eyes is simply an image that is used so we can understand the context of the psalm and, by extension, our circumstances. Squinting makes small but important things visible to the human eye. We don't squint to see something we don't care about. When God squints, it is the conscious act of allowing us to go through a trial so we can see how some stuff that we thought was small and insignificant is messing up our lives. The eyelids of God—that is, the squinting of God—try men.

Trials are never without a purpose. They always bring up to the surface behaviors, emotions, and habits that hinder your walk with God. You may think that anger against your father is no big deal. In fact, you think you've dealt with it. But God sees a tiny, scared little girl protecting herself in the corner of her heart. When He squints and allows some things to happen that bring that pain to the surface of your consciousness, you will see her, too. Those "little white lies" you tell may not be a big deal to you, but God will allow one of them to try you because He wants to destroy that deceptive, manipulative spirit in you. It wars with His very nature in you. God doesn't squint so that He can see better; He does it so you can.

The greatest comfort can be found in the image of the eyelids of God. Yes, they test you, and no, it's not always pleasant. But God never puts you through a test He hasn't taught you to pass. Remember those eyes that see your trust? He knows what your trust consists of, so He's not going to test you on anything you haven't learned about Him.

# The Anatomy of God

When I was in the sixth grade, my teacher was Thelma Jean Nickerson. When she gave a test, she would do two things: first, she would say, "Clear your desk." Then she would say, "Keep your eyes straight ahead." She'd pass out the tests, then say, "You may begin." We turned our papers over and started working. She would sit at her desk and watch us there weeping and gnashing our teeth. We were tortured, head-scratching, ponytail-pulling, struggling little balls of anxiety. And she just looked at us with the tiniest of smirks on her face that seemed to say, "What are you all waiting for? Hurry up and finish this test so I can go home."

Then she did something strange. She would get up and begin to walk up and down the aisles, looking at every student as he or she took the test. She was the meanest woman in the world to me. But one day Ms. Nickerson threw me a curve. She surprised me. To this day, I haven't forgotten it. Ms. Nickerson was walking by my desk during one of her grueling exams. Let me tell you, I was struggling. I was having a rough time with one particular problem. It didn't help that Ms. Nickerson kept walking by my desk. Was she getting some twisted sense of elation out of watching me sweat?

I decided to guess at the answer. I figured a slim chance was better than none. I did not know the answer, and it didn't look like it was going to fall out of the sky for me, so I decided to put a check in a box and get over it. I was about to put a check in the wrong box when Ms. Nickerson pointed with her finger at the right answer, then kept going.

I am stunned to this day. The woman who made the test turned around and gave me the answer to the problem in the test. Similarly, God knows when we're going through a test. He allowed the test to happen. He knows all the answers. And just when you think you can't struggle anymore and you're about to give up, He'll let the Holy Spirit come by and give you the answer. He wants you to know that every test He allows is open-book. The Bible has every answer you need, and you are allowed to use it. In fact, you're encouraged to. Only a fool would go to an open-book test and not bring the book with all the answers.

## Eyes That Look at Me

I have a question for you. When was the last time someone winked at you? Okay, now let me ask you this: What's in the winking of the eye? Sometimes the wink simply means I see you. Sometimes it means I see you and I want to see more of you. Sometimes it means I saw what you did, and I'm going to act like I didn't see it, but I want you to know that I saw it. That last one is a wink from the eye of God.

There's a lot of comfort in knowing that God sees you. However, there can also be a lot of discomfort in knowing that. I've done some things I wish God hadn't seen. We saw in our chapter on the face of God that David was bold enough to ask God not to look at some of his stuff. The knowledge that God sees me does not always make me feel warm and fuzzy— mostly because I know that while the loving-kindness of God sees me, His justice and righteousness do, too. So when I sin, I run the risk of offending the holiness of God on a day when His mercy is not as abundant as I would like it to be. That's why it's good to know that while God does see me with His eyes, there are some instances where He will merely look at me and not gaze. In those times, though, He makes it clear that He's not ignoring me or excusing me; He's just cutting me a little slack...for now. That's what the wink is all about.

*Then Paul stood in the midst of Mars' hill and said, Ye men of Athens, I perceive that in all things ye are too superstitious. For as I passed by, and beheld your*

*devotions, I found an altar with this inscription,* TO THE
UNKNOWN GOD. *Whom therefore ye ignorantly worship,*
*him declare I unto you.*                    (Acts 17:22–23)

Use your imagination. The apostle Paul went to Athens
to a place called Mars Hill to engage the men there in what
appeared to be a philosophical debate. Mars Hill was a place
in Greece where all the great minds and the great thinkers
would gather and debate. The site is still there, as a matter
of fact. There's a place in London today called the Speakers
Corner. It's similar. People go there and get up and say what
they want to say and discuss it. Speakers Corner is similar,
but it is lightweight compared to Mars Hill. That place was
known for the intellectual caliber of its philosophical orators
and expositors.

One day, Paul showed up and spoke. He gave a discourse
wherein he proposed to introduce them to the true and living
God. He told them that he had seen an inscription that read, "To
the Unknown God." He then offered to introduce them to this
God they did not know. In his speech—his sermon, really—
Paul gave us a wonderful revelation about the eyes of God.

*For in him we live, and move, and have our being; as*
*certain also of your own poets have said, For we are also*
*his offspring. Forasmuch then as we are the offspring of*
*God, we ought not to think that the Godhead is like unto*
*gold, or silver, or stone, graven by art and man's device.*
*And the times of this ignorance God winked at; but now*
*commandeth all men every where to repent.*
                                        (Acts 17:28–30)

Understand that as Paul made his way through the city
of Athens, he could not help but notice that the city was
filled with idol gods everywhere. Even today there are rem-
nants and remains of idols all over the city of Athens. So Paul

decided to go to the most public place in this city of idols and basically preach the Gospel.

He began to talk to them about God. He talked about God the Creator, who created us all out of one blood. He talked about unity within humanity and unity of origin. He pointed out that even their own poets affirmed that we are God's off-spring. By the time Paul got to verses 28 and 29, he was talking about how God is not like gold or silver or stone, something that can be shaped by art and man's devising. This "Unknown God" is the One in which we live and move and have our being. This is the God, Paul declared, that I want to introduce you to. He's a God who wants to be known. But He's not a God who was shaped by human hands.

Paul went on to explain that during those times when they were tempted to depict God with man-made idols, God merci-fully winked at them. He chalked it up to ignorance. When Paul characterized them as ignorant, they would not have taken offense because, remember, these were thinkers. To be ignorant meant simply to be unknowing or unexposed. They were anxious and open to new revelation, so ignorance was seen as an opportunity to learn. We should be more like them in that respect.

The Greek word Paul used when he said they were "igno-rant" is the same word as "unknown" written in the inscrip-tion "To the Unknown God." He was brilliantly laying out the argument that the Unknown God whom they were build-ing altars to wants to be known. But he let them know that God can't be made with human hands. They didn't know that when they built their idols, so Paul said God understood that and had been cutting them some slack because they didn't know any better. He *"winked"* at their ignorance.

Now, to wink means to overlook. God overlooked the fact that idol worship offended Him. He has been known to get pretty upset about it. But because of their ignorance, He overlooked it. The word literally means to look beyond. That is not to say that God didn't see it or make a note of it. He just chose not to blast them for it because they had not had the revelation of Him in their lives yet. With the arrival of Paul, that was about to change.

When God winks, or looks over sin, that does not imply by any means that He approves of it, ignores it, or is ignorant of it. Many of us conclude that because God overlooked our sin and did nothing, we got away with something. However, to say that God winked is to say that He did not punish us with the severity that our disobedience warranted. He didn't send His wrath, so sometimes we erroneously conclude that what we did couldn't have been too bad. That is not so. The people in Athens were breaking the first four commandments. God winked at something for which He had at other times killed folks. He winked at them when they were ignorant. But now...

Don't ever let a "but now..." catch you unawares. When you see a "but" or a "but now" somewhere, it means that what was said just before that is null and void. Paul said that God was willing to wink because of their ignorance, "but now...." That canceled two things. It canceled their ignorance, for one. They knew better now. Paul was telling them the truth. Second, it meant that the winking season was over. James said that to him who knows to do good and doesn't, it is sin. That doesn't imply that if you don't know what you're doing, it isn't sin. It means that when you do know that what you're doing is not good and you do it anyway, then you are deliberately sinning before God. Paul called the men of Athens to repentance because what they did from that point on would be a deliberate violation of God's commands, and God doesn't wink at that.

God will wink in your ignorance, but you should know that it is never His intention to leave you ignorant about anything. Remember, He is the God whose eyes see everything. He may wink at you for a while, but He will see the exact point at which you become aware of your sin. Then He will call you to repentance. You may have gotten away with it for a long time. But now…

## The Eyes That Look *for* Me

To say that God looks for us may lead us to make the mistake of assuming He doesn't know where we are. That would be true if God were human. However, the idea of God's looking for us amplifies and magnifies His almost relentless desire to move in our lives. A more accurate interpretation of "for" would be to say that God is looking "for the benefit of" or "on the behalf of" us. It is an expression of God's persistent yearning to exert influence on and in us to bring us closer to His divine will for us. There is a very graphic, very picturesque illustration of God's searching on our behalf in 2 Chronicles 16:9:

> *For the eyes of the LORD run to and fro throughout the whole earth, to show himself strong in the behalf of them whose heart is perfect toward him.*

Both behavior and intent are obvious in this Scripture. The eyes of a concerned, caring God are seeking. He's looking all over the world to and fro, back and forth, up and down, leaving no stone unturned, no cave unexplored. He's not only looking for something, but He's also looking for something to do. God's goal—to show Himself strong for His people—is the thing that drives Him to search. This is the portrait of a relentless search. God is looking, and He's not going to stop looking until He finds what He's looking for. Remember that His eyes run *"to and fro"* as He searches for someone to show Himself strong for. Now take a look at Psalm 39:6 to see another picture of *"to and fro."*

> *Surely every man walketh in a vain show: surely they are disquieted in vain: he heapeth up riches, and knoweth not who shall gather them.*

The King James Version of this verse says that man *"walketh in a vain show"* and *"they are disquieted in vain."* In the *New International Version*, it says this:

> *Man is a mere phantom as he goes to and fro: he bustles about, but only in vain; he heaps up wealth, not knowing who will get it.*

Let's look at this picture. Man here is walking to and fro. Walking usually speaks of one's conduct, lifestyle, or way of life. The writer of this psalm said that the man in this verse is one whose lifestyle is of a particular type. He said this man is walking back and forth, to and fro, in a vain show, or in vanity. He is described as a *"phantom."* That word suggests that he is a shadow, a representation of the fragility of life. It's like saying man is nothing but a mist or vapor. He's no more than a shadow.

He goes to and fro in a vain show. Imagine that our man is a traveler journeying through a desert. He's dry, he's tired, he's weary, he's thirsty, and he's hungry. Here comes the vain show. His eyes light up because off in the horizon he sees the shimmering waters of an oasis. He begins to pick up the pace and finally reaches the place where he thought the water was, but where he expected to find cool water, he discovers more sand. It was a mirage. For all its shimmering in the distance, there was no payoff. It was a vain show. And he continues this seeking and not finding throughout his desert excursion.

Here is the image of a person who spends his whole life going after stuff that never fulfills him, who has spent time, energy, resources, emotions, passion, and focus chasing things that do not matter and do not satisfy the longing and the thirst of the soul. It is a life lived to and fro in a vain show. You have seen lives like this. Some of you are living lives like this, obsessed with nothingness. The things you invested so much of your effort in have not proven their worthiness to be desired. We are addicted to the chase and unimpressed with the catch.

It is important to mention here that our motives may be pure. We are looking for something we can delight in. We want fulfillment, refreshment, and rest. Some of us search for healing, others for deliverance. There is nothing wrong with any of that. The problem is we're not finding any of that. We're looking to and fro and finding nothing of import to grab and hold on to. The bigger problem is that when we've been in the desert for a long time, we become weak and delirious. We get so desperate and thirsty that we'll take anything that looks like water and be satisfied.

That's the dangerous thing about a vain, desert life. You get weak, and when you get weak, you become prey for something or someone who has been waiting for you to get to this point. Remember that God's eyes are looking to and fro, and man is walking to and fro. Turn to Job 1:6–7, and let's see who else is in this to and fro mix.

> *Now there was a day when the sons of God came to present themselves before the Lord, and Satan came also among them. And the Lord said unto Satan, Whence comest thou? Then Satan answered the Lord, and said, From going to and fro in the earth, and from walking up and down in it.*

There it is. On the earth and going to and fro is none other than that lying accuser of the brethren, satan himself. You kind of get the idea that if satan is going to and fro, and we are going to and fro, that sooner or later we're bound to run into each other. This is not somebody we want to meet in our travels, especially when we're weak, because 1 Peter tells us what his intentions are for anyone he meets on the road.

> *Be sober, be vigilant; because your adversary the devil,*
> *as a roaring lion, walketh about, seeking whom he may*
> *devour.*                                    (1 Peter 5:8)

Man is going to and fro. Satan is also going to and fro. Man is looking for hope, deliverance, refreshment, fulfillment, intimacy, and delight. Satan is looking to devour, gulp down, and swallow man. His goal is not to wound you; his goal is to destroy you. His goal is not just to give you a bad name or to take you down a peg or two. He wants to swallow you until there is no more of you left. And he's traveling around looking specifically for you. That's the bad news.

The good news is that satan is so obsessed with you, he's not paying attention to the eyes of God. They've been following him in his to and fro, watching him watch you. The Bible says God's eyes are searching for us for the purpose of showing Himself strong to us. That phrase *"show himself strong"* (2 Chronicles 16:9) means "to attach to, to hold strongly to, to fasten to." God says when He finds a person whose heart is right, whose eyes are on Him, and who is weak in the battle, He will attach Himself to that person, and He will attach Himself so closely that He becomes the very strength that person needs. A heart that is right is not a heart that is sinless; it is a heart that has acknowledged its helplessness against sin and its hope in almighty God. God says He will meet that person in his weakness and become his strength.

Do you see the pattern? I'm looking for fulfillment and intimacy and blessings. The enemy is looking for me. God is looking at both of us, ready to come the moment I get my eyes off the blessings and put them on Him. Then He will become my strength, fight my battles, and bless me exceeding abundantly above all I could ask or think.

When I'm too weak to do for myself, I have a God whose eyes are on me, waiting for the opportunity to be strong. That said, I have the answer to the question that has gripped me since September 11. "Did You see that, God?" Yes, He saw it. He saw us when we were struck. He saw us fall. He saw every tear. He saw every man and woman beneath the rubble. He saw us weak. And He will see us through every step of this. The eyes of God see everything.

And the enemy will see us rise victorious as God attaches Himself to us and becomes our strength.

## Four

# From Your Lips: The Ears of God

Had I but serv'd my God with half the zeal
I serv'd my king, He would not in mine age
Have left me naked to mine enemies.
—William Shakespeare, *Henry VIII*

I'm not the best listener in the world. There's so much going on in my brain at any one moment that conversation is difficult to insert sometimes. It's like trying to stuff another folder into a filing cabinet that's already crammed full. *Crammed* may not be entirely accurate. That implies there's no order to it, that the information is jumbled and therefore hard to retrieve or add to. Rather, my brain is a lot like my study at home. It doesn't make sense to anyone but me. To others it looks like a mess, but I know where everything is, and I know if anything's been moved. Listening, then, is not so much an issue of having too much information as it is a storage issue.

As I looked at and examined this image of the ears of God, I must say, God's hearing is, to me, one of His more impressive features. Like His eyes, the ears of God are a lot less complicated in their operation for Him than they are for us. Our ears are comprised of three major parts: the outer, middle, and inner ear. The outer ear acts as a receiver, the middle ear is sort of an amplifier, and the inner ear functions as a transmitter, sending information to the brain where it is sorted out to tell us what we heard, where it came from, and how loud it was. God's ears hear. End of story. There's no elapsed time between something said and something heard. God hears as you say it.

Keep in mind, too, that the hearing of God, like all His other senses, is spiritual in nature. He's hearing more than just what you say. He hears what you think, what you feel, what you want, what you meant to say, what your spirit says, and what's hidden in your heart, even from you. Still, as amazing as all that is, it's not what I find most impressive.

His ears reveal something to us about His omniscience. God hears all because He knows all, and He knows all because He hears all. There are no news flashes with God. There are no surprises with Him. You don't come up with an idea, then share it with God. He already heard the idea before you came up with it. Sometimes you'll hear a person say, "From your lips to God's ears." This figure of speech speaks to the fact that there is nothing you can say that God doesn't hear.

God's hearing also speaks to His omnipresence and His omnipotence. He hears and is hearing in all places, at all times, at the same time. And there is nothing He does not have the ability to hear. The God who is all-knowing is also all-present. David said, "Where can I go to flee from Him?" (See Psalm 139.) There is not a word uttered from the lips, in the mind, or in the heart of man that God does not hear. That is awesome, but it is still not the most amazing thing about His ears to me.

The thing I find most incredible about the ears of God is the fact that He uses them to listen. God is a good listener—and He doesn't have to be. He's omniscient, omnipresent, and omnipotent. He knows everything you have said, are saying, and will say, all at the same time, and He has known it forever. But He still listens to you pray. He listens to your praise. He listens to you cry. He listens. He gives it His undivided attention, which is deep when you think about it. God can give His undivided attention to billions of people at the same time, all the time. I don't have enough pages to write about that. I have a hard enough time trying to wrap my head around the fact that God listens.

His hearing doesn't impress me as much as His listening does. In order to listen, you have to be interested, concerned, and ready to respond, but you must also be present to catch all the nuances and inflections that might indicate anything that conflicts with what's being said. God doesn't have to do any of that. He knows if you're lying or telling the truth. He knows if your heart is breaking and you're just trying to put up a good front. He knows...*everything.* But He still listens, He still encourages you to say what you have to say, and, while you're doing it, He's listening.

The book of Titus warns about idle talk. (See the *New King James Version.*) Idle talk is meaningless or worthless talk. It is talk that is not edifying. Titus says those words cry out to God. Think about that. God already heard them when you said them, but now they are crying out to Him on behalf of the people you hurt when you said them. Idle words reach the listening ears of God. God's ears picked up what you said about somebody behind his back.

James 5 says that our sins cry out to Him. Our sins have a voice, and they reach the ears of God. That's an interesting thing, for in James 5 we have a person who does something wrong to someone, and then that person tells God. I do something to you. You tell God. That's how my sin reaches God... from your lips. That is scary.

## God Hears, and He Cares

One of the most striking images of God's listening abilities is found in Psalm 102.

> Hear my prayer, O LORD, and let my cry come unto thee. Hide not thy face from me in the day when I am in trouble; incline thine ear unto me: in the day when I call answer me speedily....I watch, and am as a sparrow alone upon the house top. (Psalm 102:1–2, 7)

Understand that Psalm 102 does not begin with the first verse. It actually begins just prior to verse 1. It begins, if you're looking at your Bible, right under the number of that psalm and before the first verse. There you'll find a statement that classifies the psalm. That statement tells you something about the type of psalm you're about to sing. It would be like reading the label on a package to find out the flavor of something before you eat it. This designation gives us the "flavor" of the psalm. It is identified as *"A Prayer of the afflicted, when he is overwhelmed, and poureth out his complaint before the LORD."* I would say that is a very specific flavor.

Remember that these are songs, and this song is one that is to be sung by a person who is afflicted and overwhelmed and who goes to God about it. This song is part of a group of psalms called penitential psalms. These often had to do with repentance, like Psalm 51, for instance, but that's not the spin on this one. This penitential song is not so much a confession of sin as it is a confession or an admittance of sorrow.

Notice how the Word of God identifies the person who prays this prayer. Verse 1 says, *"Hear my prayer,"* while verse

2 asks God to *"incline thine ear."* The ears of God are called upon by a specific kind of person.

I'm going to make a disclaimer up front, since the psalmist went to such great length to classify and clarify the one for whom this particular psalm was written. I want to say this before we go any further. This psalm may not be for you. If it's not, I ask you to skip to the next chapter of this book and give me another chance. The description of the person speaking this psalm may not be you. This may not be where you are. The psalmist is very, very specific about the kind of man or woman who would pray this prayer and seek the ear of God.

The Bible says three things about this person. It says that he (1) is afflicted, (2) is overwhelmed, and (3) has some complaints. Remember, I understand if this is not you. The person praying is afflicted. That word is not as dramatic as it seems, however. It is not the extreme idea of suffering from some debilitating illness, although it certainly can include that. The word here is broader than that. It is more like sorrow. This is a prayer or a song for someone who is enduring sorrow. You might say, in today's vernacular, it is someone who is going through or is in a valley. Some of you are real cool, walking with God. You have it all together, and you never go through anything. You just hop from mountaintop to mountaintop. The valley is not where you hang out. May the Lord continue to bless you and keep you, in the name of Jesus, but four or five of us reading this book know what it's like to go through something. Let's see if we can find ourselves in this word.

Look at verse 2 of the passage. It says the afflicted person calls upon God in a day of trouble. Trouble, as I mentioned in the last chapter, presents the picture of a person who is trapped or hemmed in. It means you're in a tight place, and your back is up against the wall. You don't know which way to turn, and, even if you did, it wouldn't matter, because things are so tight, turning is not even an option. You can't go forward, back, or to the side. You'd fall down if you could, but falling requires you to move, and you can't do that. Sometimes your tight place is the only thing holding you up.

Trouble is when you're in a set of circumstances in which you feel confined and confused. You can't see your way out. You can't work your way out. You can't think, pay, squeeze, or calculate your way out. This kind of trouble brings about sorrow. If you're in this kind of trouble, this psalm's for you.

Second, the psalm refers to a person who is overwhelmed. Not only are your issues hemming you in, but they also are weighing you down. Actually, that word *overwhelmed* is related to clothing. It means to be clothed in something. This is a man or woman, a believer, whose struggles, problems, decisions, and fights in life are like a heavy piece of clothing he or she has to wear. The sorrow these people are experiencing has become a shroud. They're dressed up in sorrow. When you're clothed in something, it affects your appearance. In fact, what you really look like—your shape and appearance—is covered up by what you wear. Sorrow has an impact on how people see you.

Sorrow doesn't always look bad. Sometimes it gets all dressed up and tries to appear free from strife. You've seen people who want you to believe that all is well with them, but if you look at them long enough, you'll discover their "heaviness." You'll notice that there are some things weighing them down. You can see misery, depression, and sorrow on a person. These things live deep in the heart, but they are worn like a garment.

If a person wears sorrow for too long, sooner or later it becomes unbearable. Sooner or later he's going to begin to have some complaints. The psalm of one who is entreating the listening ear of God is the psalm of one who *"poureth out his complaint before the Lord"* (Psalm 102:1). Complaints don't have anything to do with dissatisfaction per se. This is not griping or bellyaching. This word for *"complaint"* is actually a very interesting word. It really means "groans and moans," but specifically moans and groans that are muffled. This is not the person who is vocal about his struggle. His is not an outburst of outrage. This "complainer" is going through a valley, and deep down inside he is being squeezed from all sides. He can't cry out, though, because he's all cried out. It's also possible that the pain is too deep. This person wishes he had somebody to talk to, but even if he did, he wouldn't know how to express it. The clothing of sorrow that covers this individual has become a muzzle preventing him from expressing his pain.

Have you ever been through that? Are you in a lonely season, walking through a valley by yourself? Verse 7 says, "I'm like a sparrow alone on the housetop." Here's the problem with the sparrow on the housetop. Birds sing, and you are in a predicament of pain and sorrow, but there's nobody to hear your song. So the psalmist and the sparrow simply moan their melody.

What, then, are the options of the afflicted and overwhelmed? They pour out their complaints before the Lord. They take their sorrow, their heaviness, and the moans that they cannot share. They take their loneliness and their weariness. They take their devastation and hopelessness. They take whatever weighs them down and pour it into the ear of God.

When I was a little boy, every now and then I'd get an ear infection, and my mama would send me to the store to get some oil. She called it "sweet oil." I never did taste it. I don't know how sweet it was, but mama would warm up this oil and tell me to hold my head over to the side. Then she would pour this warm oil into my ear. Now, I'm a little boy. I haven't gone to college yet, so I figured the oil would come out of my head somewhere eventually. If it went in, it had to come out. There were too many holes in my head for it not to. But it never did. In the process I discovered several things. First of all, I felt the warmth of this warm oil going into my ear. It was the weirdest feeling. Then it went away, and I always wondered where all the oil went.

A little while later, there'd be a pop, and I could hear again. The oil never came out. I learned later on in biology that the oil had been absorbed into my body, and, when it was absorbed, something happened. The psalmist said he poured his sorrow into the ear of God, and God's ears work as my ear did. His sorrow was absorbed into the very essence of the personhood of God, and when God absorbs your sorrow, you can believe something happens.

His ears are a revelation of His capacity to care.

God goes into action when I put my sorrows in His ear. The ears of God speak to the compassion of God. His ears are a revelation of His capacity to care.

## God Listens to Me

One of the most insulting things you can do to a person is ignore him, to not listen to him. I can't tell you how many relationships I've seen—how many couples I've counseled—where the complaint has been that one or both of them don't listen. I've talked to wives, and, invariably, somewhere in the conversation she'll say, "He just doesn't listen." I asked one woman, "How does that make you feel when he doesn't listen?" She said, "Insignificant."

It is a betrayal of a relationship to refuse to listen. It is unkind at best not to honor another person with your listening or to assume that you know what he is going to say before he says it, so while he is talking, you've already tuned him out, preferring to perfect your response instead. God knows what we're going to say, yet He honors us with His listening. Who are we to disrespect that discipline in our dealings with people?

Sometimes we half listen, then try to fix whatever the problem is so we don't have to listen to it anymore. Men are good at that. We often struggle with that, especially with our wives and children, because our provider/protector response kicks in. If you tell me a problem, I figure it's my job to fix it. It's a reflex. Sometimes people don't need you to fix things. They just want you to listen.

My wife has accused me—and I have been guilty—several times with, "Sweetheart, you are not listening to me." "Honey, you didn't listen to me." She was right, and I've thought about how I insulted her with my lack of consideration.

God cares enough to listen. When the psalmist said, *"Hear my prayer, O LORD,"* he was really saying, "Pay attention to my prayer, Lord." To hear in this context carries with it the interest of the person hearing as well as the intention to respond to what he hears. It is giving your undivided attention to someone. The listening attention of God is a function of His grace and His mercy. It is a function of His grace because we do not deserve His attention in any way. It is a gift freely given. It is a function of His mercy because if God hears all, then He hears my sin. The fact that He listens to me without condemning me is an expression of His mercy, which endures forever.

I used to think that I had to prepare what I was going to say to God or He wouldn't listen to me. I thought some of my prayers didn't get answered as a child because they weren't pretty enough. If you're not careful, your whole prayer life will get messed up listening to somebody else's prayers. When I was young, I was amazed at some of the prayers people would pray at my church.

# The Anatomy of God

We started our church service with a thing called devotion. Every week the "devoted brothers" would come, and if you listened to how they used to pray—not that it was bad for that time and season—it could really have you confused about prayer. There was one guy who used to pray, and he'd say, "Lord, here we come, once more and again, knee bent and body bowed, facing mother dust. Lord, we thank You that the room we slept in last night was not the walls of our grave; the bed was not our cooling board; the cover was not our winding." All that meant, "Lord, I'm sure glad I ain't dead this morning!"

Have you ever been in a situation where you just didn't have that much time? Let me tell you something. There have been some times I needed to hear from God, and I didn't have the time to go through Abraham. "It's my turn now, Lord. I need something. I need it now. I don't have time. I don't mean any disrespect, but I don't have time for that 'knee bent, body bowed.' I need to hear a word from You. I'm cutting to the chase. I'm cutting across the field. Help. Amen." That's my prayer. Has that ever been your prayer? "Help. Amen."

God is a God who desires to hear from you. Understand that. I've heard people go to God and apologize. "I don't mean to bother You, Lord...." God loves you. In this country there are more than two hundred million people. Every one of us could pray at the same time. We could speak in countless languages, dialects, and accents. And God is so much God that He won't miss or mess up a single prayer. He won't send your blessing over to somebody else by mistake. He won't forget where you are, where you've been, or where you've come from. He's a God who hears you. He hears *you.* He loves you just the way you are, and He wants to hear from you just the way you are, saying just what you have to say. You don't have to force God to hear from you. It's not about excusing

> God is a God who desires to hear from you.

yourself to Him when you pray. He's wondering why it took you so long to come to Him.

God's listening is attitudinal. It is something that represents how He feels about us. But it is not limited to His attitude. God's listening and hearing are also active. Our suffering psalmist asked God to *"Incline thine ear."* In fact, so there's no confusion, he said, "Incline Your ear *to me."* In other words, "Lord, lean this way and listen in this direction." Can you imagine it? What a great picture. Not only does God listen, but He also leans down to listen. That amazes me. We can't count high enough to number the things God has to think about, do, feel, say, exert influence over, or control in one moment of time. Yet, at every moment of our lives—all of our lives—He's available, and He is bent in our direction to listen to us. He stops to listen to us, to give us His attention.

> At every moment of our lives, God is available, and He is bent in our direction to listen to us.

The psalmist also said that God will do all this in his day of trouble. The word *day* here is not a reference to a twenty-four-hour period of time. It has to do with a specific period in one's experience. It is a season, a particular season or a defined series of moments. This is significant because it points to the fact that the individual who seeks the ear of God has a deliberate end in mind. He has a specific set of circumstances that require the ear of God. There's a crisis going on, and he needs God's ears attuned to that.

You don't just call upon God for no reason. His attention, His efforts, and His presence are not to be taken lightly. You have to be careful about how loose you are with the name of God. You don't fling it out into the heavens like it's your own name. There is power attached to the name of God. There was a movie on television once that featured a bunch of "Valley Girls." All through the movie, they kept saying, "Oh, my God," "Oh, my God," "Oh, my God," "Oh, my God," like a broken record. "Oh, my God." Be careful how cavalierly you utter "my God."

First of all, it makes the angels nervous. God has established and assigned ministering spirits who are deployed from heaven to meet the needs, the cries, and the pleas of the people of God. When you call upon God, He dispatches angels to meet the need you are petitioning Him for. Don't just randomly throw out an "oh my God." Don't tease the angels like that. They'll think somebody is going to get drafted into service. They'll be ready to go into action, thinking somebody is in some real trouble.

All I'm saying is if you don't mean it, don't say it. All kidding aside, respect the name of God. Don't call Him until you need Him, and if you do need Him, don't hesitate to call Him as many times as you think is necessary. He'll hear you, listen to you, and lean in to give you His focused attention. The author of Psalm 102 understood that. In his day of trouble, he called on the Lord. He let God know that this was a serious situation. "Lord," he cried, "this is a particularly bad time for me. The weight of my sorrow, distress, and discouragement is suffocating me. It's overwhelming me. Please, God, I need Your attention, and I need it speedily." That's right, he said *"speedily."*

## God Hears out of Time

In the day of trouble, incline Your ear. And *"in the day when I call answer me speedily"* (Psalm 102:2). I confess to you that this one really threw me. I didn't understand it for a while. One translation says, *"answer me quickly."* Our translation: "I need it right now." Have you ever gone to God with a rush order?

One time I was on the road, and I ordered some clothes. The man told me, "Bishop, we can ship it to you regular freight or as a rush order." Overnight delivery. The writer of our psalm asked God for a rush-order blessing. That almost sounded arrogant to me. You go to God and say, "Look, I need Your answer right away. Don't dilly and don't dally. I want it right quick and in a hurry." Then I thought about it. That's not only a permissible prayer; it's a reasonable one.

It speaks to the immediacy of God's hearing. I call upon Him in the earthly realm. I call to Him in the spiritual realm, for I call to Him where He is. I've called upon Him "in my day of trouble," which is to say I call Him in a specific increment of time. But God doesn't dwell in time; He dwells in eternity. So I call from my tight place in time, and I call out of time into eternity. I have taken my request in time, wrapped it up in my prayer, and then sent it from the earth realm out to eternity and into the very ear of God. When God hears my prayer, He responds quickly. He responds in a moment, in a twinkling of an eye, because He doesn't have to think about the answer. He already knew the answer before I asked the question. He heard my thoughts before I thought to pray. Sooner than right now and quicker than not yet, the answer is on the way.

Here comes the problem. God must now send the answer out of eternity and back into time to that tight place where I am. The journey from the earthly realm to the spiritual realm takes no time. The trip going in the other direction is a process. God doesn't have to process our petitions and prayers, but we are not God. We are not perfect, so He has to process His answer into us. That can take a second, or it can take a century. Only God knows.

The prayer was answered quickly. It was answered instantaneously because in God there is no delay, no tomorrow, no later on. He lives in an eternal "now." We don't, which means that a process has to take place before we can receive our answer from God.

The story of Elijah illustrates this principle well. The prophet went up to Mount Carmel for a duel with the four hundred fifty prophets of the idol god baal. Elijah and God were up against four hundred fifty prophets and their god baal. Of course, we know this was not a fair fight. With God on his side, Elijah had them greatly outnumbered, but stay with me. I have another point to make.

The goal is to see whose god is God—Elijah's God or baal. They said, "Let the God who answers our prayers by fire, let Him be God." Elijah said, "Shoot your best shot. You go first." Scripture says four hundred fifty prophets called on baal. And nothing happened.

After awhile, Elijah started to make fun of them. He said, "Well, fellas, maybe you're not calling loudly enough. Maybe your god has a hearing problem. Why don't you holler a little louder?" Elijah had set them up because he knew that baal was a god made by men. He had ears, but he couldn't hear them, no matter how long or loudly they called out.

"Tell you what, guys. Maybe if you cut yourself, you'll get some sympathy, and he'll pay attention to you. If you do something dramatic, he may be more willing to hear you." The Bible says these guys started cutting themselves and calling out as loudly as they could. Finally, 'round about evening, Elijah said, "Look, I've got to be getting home, and you boys have wasted too much of my time. It's my turn now."

The "answer" we're looking for is fire. Don't forget that. Elijah repaired the altar; then, knowing that he was expecting fire, he doused and completely saturated the altar with water. He didn't want any of those folks going home claiming that something had spontaneously combusted on the altar. He wanted there to be no mistaking where the fire came from. He soaked everything, including the wood. Then he prayed.

When Elijah called upon the Lord, the fire fell on the altar and burned up everything. But you have to understand that before Elijah opened his mouth, the fire was on the way. God heard the petition before the challenge came out of Elijah's mouth. However, they still had to wait until they prepared the altar to receive the fire that had already been sent from eternity.

When you call upon the name of the living God, He hears your prayer and answers it. The problem is that He has to get you ready for the answer. He has to prepare you for what He has prepared for you. He has your stuff. He has your blessing. You just can't handle it yet. Sometimes, though, you're not the problem. Sometimes the delay is caused by factors beyond your control.

There was a man named Daniel who prayed to God for three weeks. He fasted and prayed for twenty-one days before he got a knock on the door. It was a messenger with the answer to his prayer. "What happened? What took you so long?" You see, Daniel could ask that question because he knew he was in right relationship with God. He knew that there was nothing he was doing that would prevent God from answering him speedily. So he wanted to know what the holdup was. The messenger said, "God heard your prayer twenty-one days ago. Your answer was on the way twenty-one days ago, but as I began to approach you with the answer, the prince of Persia blocked my way." The prince of Persia was a territorial demon who was assigned to that area to keep out the blessings and the messengers of God, for when God gets ready to bless you, the devil gets nervous.

Don't you know that the devil doesn't want you to be blessed, doesn't want you to be healed, doesn't want you to overcome, doesn't want you delivered, happy, drug-free, prosperous, or promoted? The messenger said he'd been on the way with the answer for twenty-one days because God had heard Daniel's prayer the first day he prayed it. (See Daniel 10:12.) There were some delays in the answer's getting to Daniel, but God is working in the delays, too. He sent His archangel Michael to handle that delaying demon.

Your blessing, your answer from God, is on the way. What the demons don't know is that they can't stop God from answering you. God answers as soon as you pray. The demons don't get into the process until it's too late to do anything about it. All they can do is hold things up. But the more they hold up, the more prayers you send up; and the more prayers you send up, the more answers get built up; and eventually all those answers from God push their way through every attempt to delay or deflect them.

God looked at Daniel fasting and praying for twenty-one days, and then He sent Michael to get it through. He didn't send Herbert, or Sam, or Alice, or any of the other regular angels. Michael is the leader of God's army. Michael and his boys take out the serpent and his soldiers and kick them out of heaven in the book of Revelation. Every once in awhile, you ought to skip to the end of the Bible to see how the story ends. I promise it'll bless you. God sent Michael to get Daniel's answer to him.

You need to know that anywhere the enemy enters the process is too late. He's wasting his time, but he's too arrogant and hardheaded to realize it. He doesn't live outside the confines of time. God gave him his sandbox to play in, and he's not allowed to go outside of it. Every time somebody gossiped about your situation, God heard it and sent comfort, even before you got around to praying for it. The Bible says God saved your tears. That means He heard your cries before you asked Him to dry your tears. God has been sending answers to prayers your mother prayed over you as a child. Some of you don't need a blessing; you just need to hold on until your answer arrives.

# From Your Lips: The Ears of God

The ears of God hear everything. Do you want to know how to make God's ears perk up? Praise Him now for the answers that are on the way. Anybody can shout about what's going on now. I dare you to praise God about the things He's going to do. We walk by faith and not by sight, and faith pleases God. Your biggest shout should not come from what you see. You have to get to the place where you rejoice about what you know but can't see. Shout when you sign up for that first college course. Don't wait for graduation. God is listening.

> You can make God's ears perk up by praising Him now for the answers that are on the way.

I had a suitcase in my study that I didn't unpack for months. Every time I looked at it, I started praising God. I had packed that bag while we were in our old house because I knew God was going to bless us with a new home. I packed it after being turned down nine times for a loan. The answer was delayed because it had to work its way through people who didn't like what I did for a living, people who didn't like what color I was, and people who just didn't like me. But God told me to keep on seeking, keep on asking, and keep on knocking because the answer was on the way.

For a long time, I looked at that suitcase sitting in the corner of my new study in my new home. To other people, it looked like clutter, procrastination, and untidiness. But I knew better. To me it was a constant reminder that God listens to me.

It has been a few years since that season of my life. I have unpacked the bag. I had to. There is no room in my study for it. When I think about that, I'm grateful that God doesn't have any storage issues when it comes to listening to me...and I shout all over again.

Five

# Waiting to Inhale: The Nose of God

The conversion of a soul is the miracle of a moment, but the making of a saint is the task of a lifetime.
—Alan Redpath, *The Making of a Man of God*

As I approached my study on the nose of God, I must admit, I was a bit apprehensive. Frankly, it feels a little intrusive to spend a lot of time looking at somebody's nose—almost rude, really. Obviously, anytime you're dealing with the things of God you're treading on holy ground, but this is like *private* holy ground. At first I tried to play it off. Come on. It's just a nose. I consider my own nose to be average, as noses go. It's been with me for quite some time, and we don't have a lot of problems, my nose and I. But, if you think about it longer than a moment or two, a strange thing starts to happen. A nose, you soon realize, is a profoundly personal thing.

It doesn't seem like much at first—just a piece of flesh in the middle of your face. Bam. There it is. It's right smack dab in the center of the most exposed part of your body. If you were looking at your nose in the mirror right now, it would have just gotten a little bigger. Try an experiment. Have a conversation with someone and don't look him in the eyes. Look at his nose. See how long it takes for the person to ask, "What's wrong with my nose?" Looking at someone's nose is not just looking; it's scrutinizing. You've crossed personal space boundaries, and that makes people feel uncomfortable.

A nose is obvious. It's right out there for people to see. It can make or break your whole look. A woman could be sweet and shapely, but if she has a face like an angel and a nose like Jimmy Durante, some folks won't be able to get past that. That's just a fact. I know some of you are feverishly flipping through your mental archives searching for the Scripture reference about God not looking at the outward appearance but at the heart. I'll save you the trouble. It's 1 Samuel 16:7, just a few verses before the prophet anoints a little teenage shepherd boy named David to be the next king of Israel. David is described as *"ruddy, and withal of a beautiful countenance, and goodly to look to"* (v. 12). Translation: his nose was probably not a distraction. Stay with me here. I want to make a point, and if you're uncomfortable with the idea of a nose affecting the attractiveness of a person, you'll probably get it better than somebody else will.

A nose can ruin the whole appearance of a person if it is deformed or misshapen in some way. If it appears too big or too small or is crooked, it throws people off. People who don't like their noses or are self-conscious about their noses will tell you that the worst thing about having an ugly nose is you can't cover it up. It wouldn't be so bad if your nose weren't so "out there." This may seem ridiculous to you if there is nothing wrong with your nose. But the person who has had to deal with shame, derision, or rejection regarding it is not laughing with you.

Some of you may remember an old television situation comedy called *The Brady Bunch,* about an extended family of three sons and three daughters. In one of the episodes, the eldest girl, Marsha, gets hit in the face with a football and her nose gets all bruised and swollen. Now, up to this point, girlfriend Marsha was used to getting pretty much any boy in school to go out with her. In fact, her sister Jan had a little issue with that. Jan wasn't ugly or anything. She just wasn't Marsha, and Marsha was the flavor everybody wanted. Some of you have sisters and brothers like that. Some of you *are* sisters and brothers like that.

Well, in this episode, Marsha has a date with the captain of the football team. However, those plans change abruptly when the brother gets a look at Marsha's nose. He makes up an excuse and backs out of the date because he doesn't want to mess up his image by being seen in public with Marsha and her big ol' nose.

What do Jimmy Durante, Marsha Brady, and David have to do with the nose of God? Here's what I want you to see. A nose is a very obvious and prominent feature, but it's not an *important* feature. It is an important *organ.* That is, as an operating part of our anatomy, its use by and usefulness to the body is substantial. Most of us miss that. Most of us treat the nose as little more than an accessory to the face. When you describe it, you don't say, "Her nose really takes in a lot of air," or "His nose sure can smell."

> The nose is not an important feature; it is an important organ.

You describe it as a feature, by its appearance, and therefore you ascribe worth to it according to how beautiful it is to the eye. However, its function is actually what matters, for it plays an important role in the biological, physiological, anatomical, and psychological systems of our bodies.

God endures our warped perspectives and perceptions when it comes to His own nose. Like ours, His is a nose that breathes and a nose that smells. Breathing and smell-ing—they are the dullest and most mundane of pursuits. Yet within those ordinary activities, the nose of God is distinct from all other parts of His anatomy, for in it is the extraor-dinary revelation of salvation and worship. Our relationship with God, His miraculous love for us, and our expressions of adoration and appreciation to Him are reflected in the con-struction and performance of that member. Yet the majority of us have failed to get beyond the cosmetics of salvation and worship. We see them as accessories in our walk with God rather than essentials, and our efforts go into "beautifying" them before the world rather than "becoming" them before God.

Jesus said that God is seeking those who will worship Him in Spirit and in truth. God is seeking worshippers. What He's finding are pseudo-spiritual minstrels fanning imagi-nary glory above their heads and working themselves up into an emotional, ego-induced fever. He's seeking worshippers. What He's finding are singers and shout-ers. God is seeking people who want to find Him, and many of us are still too concerned about how holy our holy dance looks. Worship is deeper than that. Worship is more important than that. We should see worship, yes, but we need to know *why* people worship and learn *how* to worship. If we stop at the surface of worship, we've missed the point.

> Salvation is deeper than asking Jesus to come into your heart and getting a hug.

Salvation is deeper than asking Jesus to come into your heart and getting a hug. The grace of it goes beyond access to bless-ings from God. The mercy of it is more than a spiritual "get out of jail free" card. Your faith is not confined to what you believe, but *whom* you believe. And Jesus is more than just a little Baby or a dead Lamb.

Christianity is not a badge to be worn to church on Sunday and taken off Monday through Saturday. Salvation is to be worked out of us, not draped over us. Salvation is more important than we know. God didn't need to save us. Jesus didn't need to die. God saved us because He so loved the world, not because the world was so cute, or so talented, or so useful. Truth be told, if the anatomy of God included a neck, the world would be the pain in it. Salvation, by definition, means we have a Savior. Most of us want the salvation, but we try to relegate the Savior to the role of a divine pitchman hawking a heaven that pours out blessings whenever we yank on the lever of our faith. It's deeper than that. It's more significant than what we see.

Worship is not "good" because our prayers are lovely. Salvation doesn't "go bad" because we sinned. We look at salvation and worship as features of our relationship with God when they are actually vital to the workings of it. The nose of God shows us that our salvation and our worship are not just visual. They are functional, and that functionality can't be overlooked.

That's not to say that the concept of the nose as a feature has no place in a study of the anatomy of God. On the contrary, the prominence and position of the nose on a face, as it relates to the anatomy of God, speak to the idea that what the nose represents should be and should remain obvious and important to us. In other words, your salvation and your service should always be things you see when you look at God. They should be as plain as the nose on *His* face.

### Take a Breath

The nose is the natural pathway by which air enters the body in the normal course of breathing. Immediately a number of images present themselves in Scripture. In Genesis 2:7, God is seen breathing the breath of life into the nostrils of man.

89

Man is distinct from animals in that while all living creatures have life in them, only man has God's breath in him.

> *And the* LORD *God formed man of the dust of the ground, and breathed into his nostrils the breath of life; and man became a living soul.* (Genesis 2:7)

It says God *"breathed"* His *"breath"* into man's nostrils. Where it says God *"breathed,"* it means to inflate, to puff, to kindle, or to ignite. On the other hand, it also means to snuff out. The Bible speaks of the nostrils of God venting His holy anger against wickedness and the destruction that follows.

The word *breath* has a slightly different spin on it. This word is a Hebrew word that means "a puff" or "a wind." However, it also means inspiration, soul, and spirit. More specifically, it refers to the Spirit of God. So, in other words, God breathed His Spirit into man in Genesis 2:7. The Bible says that man was created in the image of God. God is a Spirit, and He breathed Himself into man.

If you imagine God breathing, you imagine air entering His nostrils, but it is important to know that the nose doesn't actually cause you to breathe. Biologically and anatomically, we breathe *through* the nose, not *with* it. The nose is not the organ with which the body breathes. Many people assume that breathing begins in the lungs. It doesn't. The diaphragm, which contracts and relaxes and causes the lungs to inflate and take in air, is not responsible for breathing either. No, the reason we breathe is so that our bodies can do what they were designed to do. Stay with me here.

Biologically, our bodies are designed to do one thing: live. In order to do that, our cells—the basic units of life in our bodies—need oxygen. That oxygen is carried by the blood, which is pumped throughout the body by the heart. A living body uses up oxygen. So the cells continually put pressure on the heart to send more oxygen through the blood. The heart puts pressure on the lungs to inflate. That makes us breathe. In other words, it is the need of the cells that makes us breathe. You missed that. Let me give it to you again. The cells need to live. And the need of the cells in the body to live is the reason we breathe. The blood and the heart are called into service by the need of the millions of cells that make up the body. That's why we breathe.

That's why God breathes, too.

God gave us life by breathing His breath into us. When sin entered the world, we became separated from Him, and we started dying. Like the cells in our bodies, we need His "oxygen" to live. So that need put pressure on the heart of God, and He responded by sending His Spirit, His "wind," His breath, His oxygen, if you will, through the blood of His Son Jesus. Did you know that the oxygen in your body can get to your cells only by your blood? Even though the cells of your skin are exposed to the oxygen in the air, they can't absorb it. It can come to them only through the blood. Likewise, in our spiritual lives, we have access to the "oxygen" of God only because of the blood of Jesus. Okay. Can we go a little deeper?

We inhale oxygen. We exhale carbon dioxide. If we were to breathe only carbon dioxide, eventually we would die. Carbon dioxide is what's left when a cell uses up its oxygen by living. How does the carbon dioxide leave the body? The same way the oxygen came in, through the blood. That same blood that brought us life-giving oxygen is the same blood that removes the carbon dioxide that would poison us and kill us if it were allowed to stay in our bodies. And the same blood that was shed for me on the cross washes me clean and takes away the poison of sin in my life.

Every once in awhile, I make my way to the gym to get a little workout in. It doesn't take long before I start breathing a little harder and a little deeper. That's because something is happening to the cells of my body. They are using up oxygen faster than normal. That means carbon dioxide is being produced at a faster rate. Higher than normal levels of carbon dioxide in our bodies automatically trigger that increased breathing. In other words, the heart is trying to get more oxygen to the cells, so we breathe harder.

The parallel between that and the breathing of God is this: increased oxygen use through exercise means more regular and efficient elimination of carbon dioxide. If we liken oxygen to the Spirit of God and carbon dioxide to sin, then when we exercise ourselves unto godliness according to Paul's exhortation in 1 Timothy 4:8, we use or incorporate more of the Holy Spirit into our living, and the sin that that effort brings to the surface can be more efficiently carried away by the blood.

You were not created the way you were by accident. God did not just grab a handful of dust off the ground, mix it with a little spit, mold you into a form, and call you man. God is a God of all wisdom. He doesn't waste anything, and He certainly didn't waste anything when He made you.

God made our bodies to reflect His glory. God is love, which means His glory is seen in His love. First John 4:9–10 tells us how God loves us. Let's look at it in the *New Living Translation*:

> *God showed how much he loved us by sending his only Son into the world so that we might have eternal life through him. This is real love. It is not that we loved God, but that he loved us and sent his Son as a sacrifice to take away our sins.*

Did you know that the very biological makeup of your body carries the story of salvation? You must see, man and woman of God, that your body is more than just a miracle of science. It is a miracle of Elohim and I AM. You are a miracle of the King of Glory, the Lord of Hosts, the Creator of all things. God has person- *The very biological makeup of your body carries the story of salvation.* ally designed and crafted everything on you and in you. And no artist presents a work that he has not signed. That's why God has deposited in your DNA His signature, which is the story of His love for you, of your salvation. I don't care who your parents are. You were a miracle to God before your father ever met your mother.

When you look at yourself in the mirror, you need to know that *"fearfully and wonderfully made"* (Psalm 139:14) are not just words that a psalmist threw in a song. That phrase literally means that when God made you—when He knitted your arms and legs together in your mother's womb—He just looked at you and said, "Mmm, mmm, mmm. What a wonder!" That is what you are to God.

Now you have to remember that there is no time between God's getting an idea and then His making that idea happen. In fact, in the unfathomable depths of His will, God wants something, decides to make it, then makes it and is pleased with it all at the same time, and He does it just by speaking. If you really think about this, it'll make you shout. God just said your name, fell in love with you, made you, and declared you "wonderful" all in the same moment. God did that. I don't care what anybody else told you about yourself. God says you're a wonder. And He put the biology in you to back it up.

Your physical body reflects the miracle of salvation. That's why you can't treat your body like it doesn't matter. Your body was designed to live, but it was purposed to glorify and honor God. Every breath you take should remind you that you live only because God loves you; and because He loves you, He saved you; and because He saved you, you ought to live for Him. When was the last time you thanked God for breathing life into you? When was the last time you gave Him credit for that?

The nose of God speaks to the choice that God made to give us life and sustain it. You can't talk about a nose without talking about breath and life any more than you can talk about the nose of God without mentioning Jesus, the Holy Spirit, and salvation.

*God's nose speaks to the choice that God made to give us life and sustain it.*

### The Flip Side...

The nose not only allows air into the body, but it also protects the body by controlling the content of the air that comes in. Dust and particles, for example, come into the nose and then get trapped by little hairs in the nose called cilia. When we blow our nose, that action eliminates those particles from the body before they've had a chance to do any damage. God "blows" His nose to protect and deliver His people from danger at the hand of their enemies.

In Exodus 15:8 God parted the Red Sea with "a blast" of His nostrils so Israel could walk through on dry land. Then, in verse 10, the same nose blew the water back down and drowned the Egyptians. Psalm 18 is a song written by David when the Lord delivered him from his enemies, particularly Saul. He said the blast of God's nostrils was a rebuke to them, or a scolding.

The word for blast is a dramatic picture word. It's the image of a stallion snorting. Anger is often typified by heavy breathing, especially through the nose. In Proverbs 22:24 we are cautioned not to make friendship with an *"angry"* man. That word for angry literally means "breathing place," and it's the same word used for "nose." Have you ever seen somebody who's really mad? His nostrils start to flare, and he breathes hard. That's what this is a picture of, only it's a little more intense.

# Waiting to Inhale: The Nose of God

The breath of God's nostrils is nothing to play with. When He's mad, He's not just standing around snorting while the angels decide to cut a wide path around Him until He cools off. His anger and His breathing are always intentional and directed. If He's mad at you, He's coming to get you, and you can forget about running or hiding from a God who sees and knows everything.

Remember that breathing is a function of the need of the cells in our bodies, not an action or choice initiated by the nose. When God gets angry, He always has a reason, and the reason always has to do with the need of God's people. Wrath is ignited in the nose of God when His people are oppressed or persecuted by their enemies. Then He will move because they need deliverance.

There is a flip side to the nose of God as it relates to the anger of God. In Isaiah 65, God is responding to Israel's prayer for deliverance from their enemies. In the chapter before that, the people want God to show up and defend them the way He had in the past. They even got dramatic with it. They said, "Oh, that You would rend the heavens! That You would come down, that the mountains would shake at Your presence! Come on, Lord! Bring fire with You when You come, hot enough to make water boil, and make Your name known to Your adversaries, that they might tremble!" In other words, "Lord, we want You to put some fire in Your pocket and come on down here and put on a show so our enemies will be shaking in their sandals, You know, like You used to do."

I love Israel because Israel would try to get God to move by calling Him on what He promised, like they could catch Him slacking. They implied—they didn't come right out and say it—that God wasn't treating them, His chosen people, any differently than He was treating the heathens. "Well, we *thought* You *said* something about us being Your people. We remember something about 'never leaving us or forsaking us.' Hmm.

We're feeling mighty lonely down here, God. We're not saying we're forsaken per se, but You have been a little absent."

Don't be too hard on Israel. We do the same thing. "God, You said You would open up the windows of heaven if I brought You my tithe. Now, I'm not saying You lied, and I haven't checked the weather channel, but so far—I'm not saying it won't happen, but so far—I haven't seen any blessings raining from heaven. Oh, and by the way, *Father,* I do recall that You said something about giving me 'whatsoever I ask.' Maybe my husband got held up in the mail. I know You have the tracking numbers from my prayers—all six hundred of them—could You check on that for me? Appreciate it."

What Israel and a few of us fail to remember is that God's goal is to make us holy, not happy. Israel was praying for God to honor His relationship with them, and all the while they were still practicing idolatry, breaking the law, and being self-righteous and prideful. They were looking to be delivered from their enemies, and they needed to be delivered from their sin.

I love how God responds to them. They want God to come out of heaven and vent His anger. They're looking for God to work up a few good blasts of air in His nostrils and let them fly in the direction of their enemies. But look what God says in Isaiah 65:1–5:

> *I am sought of them that asked not for me; I am found of them that sought me not: I said, Behold me, behold me, unto a nation that was not called by my name. I have spread out my hands all the day unto a rebellious people, which walketh in a way that was not good, after their own thoughts; a people that provoketh me to anger continually to my face; that sacrificeth in gardens, and burneth incense upon altars of brick; which remain among the graves, and lodge in the monuments, which*

*eat swine's flesh, and broth of abominable things is in
their vessels; which say, Stand by thyself, come not near
to me: for I am holier than thou. These are a smoke in
my nose, and a fire that burneth all the day.*

God's charge against Israel is this: first, they have gone
through the motions of being His people, but it all has been
superficial. That's what He meant when He told them that
they *"sought"* Him but *"asked not"* for Him. To seek means
"to research or inquire after." It is also a word that implies
worship. Asking in this context means "to beg, entreat, or
borrow." In other words, Israel was "playing church." They
were coming into the building, doing all the posturing and
pretending they needed to do to look holy, but they weren't
seeking an audience with God. They weren't asking Him to
meet their needs, change their lives, or honor them with His
presence.

They liked being called God's chosen people, but they didn't
want to live like God had chosen them. They were bold about
it, too. God said they were provoking Him to anger continually to His face. And God told them that everything they've
been doing—He gave them a laundry list of their offences—
has been *"a smoke in my nose, a fire that burneth all the day."*
Now watch this, because there is a very important revelation
regarding the working out of your salvation in this specific
characterization of the nose of God.

Israel was in rebellion. They had broken the law, and God
said their relationship with Him was superficial. It didn't have
any substance. Remember, Israel had just asked God to come
down out of heaven and show Himself to their enemies. That
sounds like they had faith in God, but God said they didn't.
Why? Because faith that is seen is not faith. "Faith is the substance of things hoped for, the evidence of things *not seen*"
(Hebrews 11:1). They were asking God to do what He had

already done so they could look like chosen people to their enemies. Their concern was with the cosmetics of being God's people, not with the character that comes along with being God's people. They were asking God to put on a show so they could look good. Have you ever asked God to do that?

Have you ever looked at your circumstances and asked God to deliver you from them because you were ashamed of how bad you were looking to other people? Are you asking God for a husband because you are embarrassed about your singleness? Why are you praying about your weight? Are you asking God for a car because you're ashamed of riding the bus? Have you ever wondered if you look "saved" enough to people?

God will allow difficult situations into our lives to build character in us, but many of us don't want the character. We just want the cosmetics. We want to look like some Scriptures, but not all of them. We'll wear a "God's Property" T-shirt, but I don't see anybody standing in line to get the T-shirts that say "I know Him in the fellowship of His sufferings" or "Obedience is better than sacrifice" or "Though He slay me, yet will I trust Him." You don't see those T-shirts because they are not worn on the skin. They are worn on the heart.

A superficial relationship with God is a smoke in His nose that burns all day long. That paints a very specific picture. It means that there is a continual irritation in the nostrils of God, a nonstop annoyance. It's like there is something in His nose that He can't get out, and it's bugging Him; it's ticking Him off. God is saying that superficial relationships irritate Him. They get on His nerves.

Here's the point. God said that Israel's insincerity and the shallowness of their relationship with Him were a constant nose irritation to Him. If you've ever gotten too close to the barbecue pit and breathed some of the sooty smoke through your nose, you understand what God is saying here. The smoke in His nose aggravated and irritated the inside of His nostrils. Where did the smoke come from?

The book of Revelation says the prayers of God's people are offered up to God as incense. (See Revelation 5:8.) The altar of incense in the Old Testament tabernacle was the place where the morning and evening prayers were offered along with sacrifices. Incense is burned, and it is burned for its fragrance. Prayers are incense, and those that are accepted by God are called a "sweet savor" in His nostrils. The Lord's words to Israel in Isaiah 65 were a response to the prayers they sent up in Isaiah 64. But whereas the incense of prayers that are acceptable to God is a sweet aroma, the smoke of Israel's supplications was a burning in His nostrils.

What do you do when there is something in your nose that is annoying and frustrating you? That's right; you got it. You blow your nose. And that's what God did. He got angry. If you read the rest of Isaiah 65, you'll find out that God vented His anger at Israel and told them all that He planned to do to them because of their rebellion.

God is not above blowing His nose at us. Jesus didn't die on that cross so we could work out our salvation on a part-time basis. Paul told us to exercise ourselves unto godliness. That means we have to make a choice to sweat a little and put some effort into becoming the people that God has called us to be. Some of us eat the Word in awesome, Spirit-filled, Bible-believing churches. We pile our plates high every Sunday and throw in a little Bible study and conference hopping on the side. And we become pew potatoes. We've gotten fat and happy, but not holy. God says we think we're "holier than thou," but that's far from the truth. God says that makes His nose burn.

You will recognize it when God blows His nose. He will allow some things to come into your life that will make you act on all those Bible verses you've been naming and claiming, blabbing and grabbing. He'll make you sweat. He'll allow you to go through some stuff that uses up everything you know about Him but didn't act on. He'll humble you. Sweat. He'll put you in a tight place. Sweat. He'll let them dog you out at work. Sweat. And when you've come to your senses and offer up your broken spirit and contrite heart instead of that fake and phony fluff that only impresses the people in the front row, He'll be there…to breathe some more of Himself into you. He loves you that much. He loves you too much to let you continue on a path of mediocrity. You serve an excellent God, and He will not stop until all the excellence He put in you is worked out in you. The nose of God should make you remember that, because you're His son or daughter, He loves you enough to chasten you.

There's something very interesting about the human nose that I want you to see. The nose is connected to the middle ear via a structure called the eustachian tube. The eustachian tube equalizes air pressure on both sides of the eardrum. That's why, in an airplane, a change in cabin pressure will cause your ears to stop up. There's nothing actually in your ear but air, and "popping" your ears is just the act of relieving pressure. However, it's not just a change in pressure from the outside that can have this effect on your ears. You can change the air pressure in the eustachian tube by blowing your nose too hard or by having an illness or infection that blocks your nasal passages. The pressure that is put on the eardrum can make it difficult to hear.

I want to suggest to you that there is a cycle that occurs in this scenario with Israel in Isaiah 65 that further illuminates our understanding of the nose of God. God's words to Israel in Isaiah 65 were a response to their prayers in Isaiah 64. God called their prayers a continual burning in His nose. I want to suggest to you that the same thing that occurs in our noses occurred with God regarding Israel, and that it could and does occur with us.

Israel was in continual rebellion. That filled the nostrils of God with a burning smoke that was continually irritating Him. I want to suggest to you that continual, habitual sin pollutes the nasal passages of God and can negatively impact His hearing. In other words, continual sin keeps God from hearing our prayers. When God is said to "hear" prayers, it means He has decided to accept them and answer them. We may be stretching this metaphor to an unreasonable length, but I am reminded of several passages that suggest the same thing.

*If my people, which are called by my name, shall humble themselves, and pray, and seek my face, and turn from their wicked ways; then will I hear from heaven, and will forgive their sin, and will heal their land.*

(2 Chronicles 7:14)

*I cried unto him with my mouth, and he was extolled with my tongue. If I regard iniquity in my heart, the Lord will not hear me: but verily God hath heard me; he hath attended to the voice of my prayer. Blessed be God, which hath not turned away my prayer.*

(Psalm 66:17–20)

*Likewise, ye husbands, dwell with them according to knowledge, giving honour unto the wife, as unto the weaker vessel, and as being heirs together of the grace of life; that your prayers be not hindered.* (1 Peter 3:7)

*Therefore if thou bring thy gift to the altar, and there rememberest that thy brother hath ought against thee; leave there thy gift before the altar, and go thy way; first be reconciled to thy brother, and then come and offer thy gift.* (Matthew 5:23–24)

*Therefore take unto you now seven bullocks and seven rams, and go to my servant Job, and offer up for yourselves a burnt offering; and my servant Job shall pray for you: for him will I accept: lest I deal with you after your folly, in that ye have not spoken of me the thing which is right, like my servant Job.* (Job 42:8)

In that last passage with Job, we clearly see the image of prayer as an offering that is accepted in the presence of God. Offerings, both animal and incense, were always made at an altar. The combination of the incense and the altar represents the sufficiency of the sacrificial death of Christ. We would not have access to the presence or the grace of God were it not for the shedding of His blood.

## Only Because of the Blood

Here is the final thing I want you to see that is revealed to us by the nose of God. We are accepted by God and before God only through Jesus. That is our salvation. In John 1:29 John the Baptist declared that Jesus is *"the Lamb of God, which taketh away the sin of the world."* Jesus is called the *"propitiation for our sins"* (1 John 2:2). That means He took our place and accepted death on the cross for every sin that was or will ever be committed, making it possible for us to be allowed into the presence of God and ultimately to receive the gift of eternal life with God.

That is not a small thing. Don't treat it like that. If I threw you out of the path of a speeding car, you would thank me and perhaps even reward me. But I would have saved only your body. Jesus rendered your earthly body obsolete, and He alone is the reason you will become a new creature. He was the only

Sacrifice acceptable to God to atone for the sins of the entire world. As with the cells in our body, the blood means the difference between life and death for us.

As I said before, God did not save you to bring you to heaven to keep Him company. He is not lonely. Romans 8:29 says you were predestined *"to be conformed to the image of his Son, that he might be the firstborn among many brethren."* You were saved so that you would become like Jesus. You do that by doing what He did.

> *I beseech you therefore, brethren, by the mercies of God, that ye present your bodies a living sacrifice, holy, acceptable unto God, which is your reasonable service.*
>
> (Romans 12:1)

There's our image again, only now, because of Christ, we become the offering unto God. God desires that we would offer more to Him than just our prayers. He wants us. That word *service* is actually a word that means "worship," and it specifically implies sacrificial worship. God wants us to *be* worship, not just *do* worship. We offer, and we are the things that are offered. Did you get that? Our body is the sacrifice, but we sacrifice our body. Now, being a sacrifice can be faked. You can look like you've given your life to God all day long. However, here God says He wants you to make a choice, too. The sacrifice is not complete until you make an internal decision to give your life to God. You can't fake that.

That's where that word *reasonable* comes in. It means "pertaining to reason." It implies that your service, or worship of God, is not something you just feel or emote. It is worship that reflects and assumes intelligent devotion to God. Worshipping God should make sense to you. When people see your relationship with God, they should believe that you made a good choice, not that you make good church entertainment. If you love God, you ought to know why. If you believe God is worthy, you ought to know why. If you're hollering, "Thank You, Jesus!" at the top of your lungs, that's okay. Just know why.

In this passage God is asking for all of you—body, mind, and spirit. Your worship is about your spirit because, as I said at the beginning of this chapter, God is looking for spiritual worshippers. Its reasonableness includes your mind. What you're offering is your body, and that offering is acceptable to God only because of what Jesus did for you. There is a divine connection between your salvation and your worship.

Because of what Christ did for you, you are able to be like Him and offer the sacrifice of yourself to the Father. And because of the blood of Christ, you become an acceptable sacrifice. You can become, thanks to Jesus, the sweet savor of a sacrifice that is pleasing to God. The same nose that breathed life into you now breathes in the wonderful fragrance of your offering of yourself to Him.

You can't smell without breathing, and you can't breathe without smelling. Likewise, you can't have salvation without worship, and you can't have worship without salvation. He died to save you. Salvation. You live to become a sacrifice. Worship. He had to die so you could live. Now you have to die so He can live in you. It's only reasonable.

Your nose is a prominent and obvious feature on your face. It helps to define the whole look of you. But if you get caught up in the way it looks, you'll miss its real beauty, which is its purpose and function. The nose is connected to all the other sensory organs in the face—to the ears, eyes, and mouth. It is designed to protect those organs and the rest of the body by filtering and carrying out dust and other debris. It has direct connections to the centers in the brain that affect mood, emotion, and memory. You can smell something, and it will bring back wonderful memories, change your mood, and evoke vivid, passionate emotions.

# Waiting to Inhale: The Nose of God

When you look at the nose of God and see the visible man-ifestations of His love for you, like His provision and pro-tection, you ought to remember that that's just a small thing compared to the real beauty of your salvation and worship. You ought to remember how all God's senses are called into service on your behalf. You ought to know that His protection includes not allowing the debris of sin to remain in your life. Most important, when you look at the nose of God, you should know that your sincere, holy, reasonable worship, made pos-sible by your salvation, is inhaled by God and evokes passion-ate and powerful emotions and feelings...about you. Ask God to tell you what He thinks of you sometime. Every once in awhile, He'll speak into your spirit and say, "Mmm, mmm, mmm. What a wonder!"

Six

# A Word from the Wise: The Mouth of God

If words are to enter people's hearts and bear fruit, they must be the right words shaped so as to pass men's defenses and explode silently and effectually within their minds.
—J. B. Phillips, *Making Men Whole*

The mouth of God is the most engaging of all His features. Of all the parts of His anatomy, this one is the most complete reflection of His personality. That He speaks at all says a lot about Him. He's God. In Him is everything. He's never lonely because He always has Him, and He's always enough. Does He really have to speak? What is He going to say that He doesn't already know? And yet He opens His mouth and life occurs, because that's all that could spring forth out of Life Himself.

I am amused at the depictions of His conversation in film and television. Usually there's a booming, bass-infused voice of authority accompanied by thunder, lightning, and quaking earth for emphasis. It's no wonder people are scared to get to know Him. Not that those images are completely wrong, mind you. If anyone deserved whirlwinds and falling mountains as punctuation for His discourse, it would be God. But we do Him and ourselves a disservice when we limit our understanding of His dialogue with us to violent, dramatic outbursts or ominous threats of wrath and impending destruction. There is more to the mouth of God than that. There is more *in* the mouth of God than that.

The mouth of God reveals the intentions and priorities of God. We've all seen or heard of encounters between fathers and the young men who desire to date their daughters. Dad is stern and unsmiling as he asks, "Son, what are your intentions toward my daughter?" He wants to know, up front, today, what this boy's plans are for his cherished progeny. When I was a young man, I didn't understand that question. My intentions? I *intend* to go the show and maybe get a burger later on.

*The mouth of God reveals the intentions and priorities of God.*

What I later learned, having two daughters of my own, is that the question is designed to establish a covenant of trust between the father and the young man. You want it understood (I'm speaking as a father now) that you are about to let him walk out the door with something that is of great value to you. You explain to (*warn*) him that you are expecting him to return it to you in the same or better shape. Then you give him a serious (*threatening*) look and ask, "Young man, what are your intentions?" If you've done your job right, the boy will be eager (*too afraid not to*) to tell you the truth.

God has made you a steward over your life. Then one day He asked you to give it to Him. Your first question to God may have been, "What are Your intentions for me?" You are of great value to you. Some of us know what it's like to be abused and broken, and we're not in a hurry to hand ourselves over again just because someone asked. So we want to know, "God, what are Your intentions?" Unlike the aforementioned young man, God doesn't have to be intimidated into telling us the truth. He is Truth. He also understands our concern for our "treasure," so, in order to ease our minds, God has told us, from His mouth, all His intentions.

He intends to love us. He intends to protect us. He intends to bless us and grace us with His presence. He intends to discipline us and correct us. He does not intend to return us to ourselves. He intends to keep us. And His intentions are for us to be in better shape than we were when He got us. All this God has said to us, gently, tenderly, in His Word.

It's hard to attach a lot of versatility to the mouth of God. It speaks. Our mouths smile, but God's doesn't in the sense that ours do. His "smile" is a shining of His face. Because God is the Source of all joy, He doesn't need to smile. He *is* a smile. Our mouths eat and chew. He is self-existent and doesn't take anything in, for everything is already in Him. Our mouths kiss and express and emphasize our emotions. God speaks with His.

At first glance you might be tempted to think that God's mouth is more limited in its operation than yours is. But when you consider His words, countless facets unfold before you. Our mouths say words. God's mouth says His Word, and He is His Word. So then, when the mouth of God speaks, what comes out is God. His words are as creative as He is, as powerful as He is, as life-giving as He is, and as life-changing as He is. His emotions are wrapped up in His words. Because He is love, all the words that He speaks are love. They may not always sound that way to us, but, remember, the mouth of God is the revelation of the intentions and priorities of God.

The mouth of God has been used in several idioms, metaphors, and figures of speech that all refer to some dynamic of reaction by God. Several times in Scripture you will find the phrase "to inquire at the mouth of God." To inquire at the mouth of God is to consult God for His will, His direction, or His guidance. It means to seek counsel from God. The "rod" of the mouth of God speaks of God's divine rebuke. The "judgment" of God is a manifestation of the wrath of God most often upon His enemies. "Judgment of God" is also a synonym for the law and the word and the will of God.

Several times in Scripture we find "fire out of the mouth of God," which is one reflection or example of the heated anger of God. The nose, which we covered in the previous chapter, is another one. And there are twenty-four instances in the Old Testament where "according to the mouth of God" occurs. Eighteen of those twenty-four references are in the book of Numbers, meaning there is a heavy concentration of that phrase in the Pentateuch, or the Torah, which is the law of God. That is, the first five books of the Bible—Genesis, Exodus, Leviticus, Numbers, and Deuteronomy—contain the most occurrences of "according to the mouth of God." The law was a revelation of God's will and God's command, given from His mouth.

As we consider the mouth of God, I want to focus our attention on two broad categories: the speaking of God's mouth and the words of God's mouth. How and why God speaks is indivisible from His words, and all His words carry with them the unmistakable stamp of His objective and purpose for speaking.

## God Speaks

God is not a God who is silent. He speaks, and He is speaking. He speaks actively and continuously and always with a reason. God's mouth is never idle. He doesn't engage in useless conversation and insincere sentiment. His reasons for saying what He does are varied, but they all have a common under-pinning, which is His relationship with His creation.

God speaks, first of all, to exhibit and express His relation-ship with creation. Genesis 1:1 says, *"In the beginning God...."* By the way, the Bible never argues the existence of God. It does not debate it. The Bible assumes the presence of God with its very first words, *"In the beginning God."* That's a revela-tion right there. The beginning is the start of something, but in order for anyone to have been there "in the beginning," he would have had to be there before "the beginning" began. God never began. He always has been, but in His eternal exis-tence, He started a clock called time.

In the beginning, God, who created beginning from being, began creating something from nothing. He did it by speak-ing. God's relationship with His creation commenced when He opened His mouth and spoke it into existence. The Bible says, *"and God said,"* *"and God said,"* *"and God said"* over and over. *"And God said, Let there be light"* (v. 3). He did not stutter. And light *was*. No debate, no argument. God didn't have to ask light to be. He didn't have to call light to the side and have a conversation with light. There were no negotia-tions going on. God did not have to bribe light to come. He did not tell light, "Look, I'll tell you what. If you come, I'll give you twelve dollars a day. I'm giving night the same deal. That's a buck an hour. Deal? Deal. I'll call you out in a minute. Don't make Me call you twice." No, God had no such discussion with light. When God said, *"Let there be,"* there was.

It is such an unimaginable concept that we struggle with it. We strain to embrace the truth that something came out of nothing because the mouth of God spoke it into being. There was nothing—no color, no time, no long or short, straight or curve, measure, depth, direction, or even *space*. How did He know what to make? There was no language. How did He know what to say when He spoke? There was no expression, only existence. How did He know *to* say anything? How did He not "begin"? And before long, it's all too much for us. We go back to where it last made sense to us.

God created all things by His mouth, and He created relationship with all things by His mouth. What is created is always defined by, limited by, and subject to the releases and restrictions placed on it by its creator. God created all things, and He decided what all things were, how they would live, and how long they would live. He created their relationships with each other as well as the boundaries within those relationships. Lions and elephants can live in the same place, but they can't have babies together. Fish can live in water but not on dry land. Some animals can swim, but they can't live underwater. By the word of God's mouth, we cannot converse with a giraffe, but we can speak to each other. God said we would multiply, and we do. All things were made by the words of God's mouth. And all things do what they do because God spoke that as well.

It is interesting, then, that so much of what He says to us is questioned. If God spoke you into existence, does He not know what you can and cannot do? Do you think a cheetah who sees a gazelle ever says, "Nah, forget it. I can't catch him, and even if I did, would he let me eat him?" Do trees ever worry that they won't bear fruit, or that there will be enough fruit? That seems silly, doesn't it? Have you ever questioned your ability to do what God has already said you can do? Let's not even consider your ministry, your relationships, or anything else that is specific to your life. What about holiness, obedience, or faith? Aren't these spoken from the mouth of God as disciplines we are to pursue? How many times does God have to tell you what He wants you to do before you believe Him, much less obey?

# A Word from the Wise: The Mouth of God

Not only were we brought into being by God's word, but we also grow in relationship with Him through His Word. He enhances our relationship with Him. Look at what Jesus said in John 14:21.

> *He that hath my commandments, and keepeth them, he it is that loveth me: and he that loveth me shall be loved of my Father, and I will love him, and will manifest myself to him.*

You can't go much further without getting that into your spirit. The person who has the Word of God and who is not only a hearer but a doer of it as well—this person is the one whom Jesus and the Father love. And it is this person to whom Jesus promised to manifest Himself. Did you get the chronology? Watch the sequence and the progression of the text. You know what God said, you do it, and then Jesus manifests Himself.

The word *manifest* is very important. It means "to shine forth," "to reveal," or "to make visible." It means to present oneself in the sight of another. It means you are conspicuous. Jesus said that if you know the Word and obey it, He will become conspicuous in your life. God's presence in your life will be obvious.

But manifestation has a second dynamic to it. The word also means "to declare," "to speak to," "to make known," and "to make known by speaking." So the Bible says that the person who has the Word and does the Word will be rewarded with the blessing of another word from God.

Many of us are waiting on God to speak about what He has not done in our lives, and God is waiting on us to do what He has already spoken about. God says He'll reveal Himself to those who are already walking in obedience. The paraphrase of that is to walk in the light that you have. God never expects you to obey what He has not told you to do. You cannot obey what you don't know to obey. But as you walk in the truth that you have and are obedient to what you already know, God reveals to you what you don't know. You are not in a position to receive what you don't know until you do what you know to do.

You can get in a car and drive from California to New York, but in the nighttime you will get there only a few feet at a time because your headlights will shine only about fifteen or twenty feet in front of your car. Your headlights will not shine from California to New York. If you stand in California waiting for God to shine a light from L.A. to New York, you'll be standing in L.A. until the cows come home—no, you won't. Even after the cows are home and in their beds asleep, you'll still be there.

God gives you enough light to take you just a little distance at a time, and sometimes you can go only as far as the light you have. Those of you trying to take a giant step, you're going to miss it, because what God wants to show you is in the little steps. You want a wife? Stop speaking to that woman who's somebody else's wife. Only then can God set you up to receive the revelation of the one who's for you. When you obey, God speaks up. He'll promote you when you perform. There is no "automatic pass" in His educational system. Until you learn the present lesson, you'll take the test for it over and over again. When you have it licked, He'll move you on to the next thing. Don't ask God to anoint you for algebra when you won't do your multiplication tables.

God says He will speak more as we respond to what He has already said. So His speaking to us is not only to enhance and express relationship; it is also purposed to involve us in our relationship with Him. As I said before, God doesn't speak without a reason. But what God says when He speaks is just as significant as whom He speaks to. If He has spoken to you, that's because His words are for you. It is never an accident when God's words reach you. You don't just happen to hear the Word of God. It is God's plan to involve us with Him. When He speaks, we are expected to listen. And that listening is an active listening. God doesn't define hearing the way we do. He considers our hearing complete when we respond to what He has said.

Fifteen times Jesus said, "He who has ears to hear, let him hear." Seven of those fifteen occurred in the book of Revelation where He added, "He who has ears to hear, let him hear what the Spirit says to the church." God is a God who speaks, and He speaks to involve us in our relationship with Him. So He says, "I speak. You hear."

Exodus 20 is a great illustration of how most of us are. God had spoken to Moses on Mount Sinai. He had given him the Ten Commandments. They were not the Ten Suggestions or the Ten Additional Optional Extras. He did not put a question mark on the end of any of them, or preface them with, "Look, if you guys have a mind to...." When God spoke His law, it was a revelation of His intentions for them and His stated priorities concerning them. Pick up the story at Exodus 20:19. Moses had just come down off the mountain. The people had been looking up at the mountain. They witnessed the lightning flashes, the sound of the trumpet, and the smoke, and when the people saw it, they trembled and stood back. By the time Moses got to them, they were pretty convinced that God was not playing with them.

> And they said unto Moses, Speak thou with us, and we
> will hear: but let not God speak with us, lest we die.

There is a problem with this. First of all, these were the people of God, and they didn't want to talk to God. They wanted the man of God to do it and then relay any messages from God. "Moses, go on up the mountain. Let us know what

God said, and we'll do it." Second, they had no plans to obey Moses because every time Moses told them what God had said, they fought him and murmured against him.

Now, you have to give them credit. They weren't stupid. If you're Israel and you have a choice between getting instructions from God or Moses, you should pick Moses every time. They knew they weren't going to obey even if they wouldn't admit it. So it would be easier to dispute and argue with Moses because Moses couldn't turn them into dust.

Some of you, not all of you, but some of you have made yourselves comfortable with a preacher being your Moses. You open your Bibles once every seven days on Sunday to find out from someone else what God has to say to you. Some folks have made themselves complacent concerning their relationship with God because they figure that as long as they show up and sit in their seats, like clockwork, the man or woman of God will come down from the mountain with their word from God. Part of the reason is that many churches don't teach people the importance of having a personal relationship with God. Some people don't know that they can get to the throne without permission from their pastor and that God is anxiously awaiting their arrival.

However, others of you are like Israel. You don't want to talk to God because you know that when you do—when you allow God to speak with you and you alone—something will have to die. You can argue with a pastor. You can debate with a preacher. You can disagree with him and go on about your business. But once you have a personal, intimate encounter with God, there are some things in your life that He's going to kill off. He's not going to allow you into His presence with your sin. As soon as He tells you that some things have to die, you can forget about the next level with Him until you obey.

# A Word from the Wise: The Mouth of God

When there are bad habits, relationships, and sinful behaviors in our lives that we don't want to rid ourselves of, we don't want to get too close to the Word of God. And we certainly don't want to get in His presence and have Him start killing off stuff. Brother, you have a choice. Sister, here are your options. You can let the truth of the Word of God begin to kill off those things that hinder your relationship with Him and keep you from being holy. Or you can watch the blessings of relationship with Him die. You can let Him kill your deceitful tongue, or you can watch your anointing die. You can let Him kill that unsanctified affair, or you can watch your peace die. You can let Him kill that drug habit, or you can watch your joy die. You can let Him kill your pride, or you can watch your vision die. He's trying to speak life into you—abundant life—and you want to trade that for deadness?

## His Words Are Life

If you go to the mountain yourself and let die what needs to die, you will find that God has been waiting for an opportunity to show you what He can do in your life. God is not only a God whose word can make life from nothing. Remember, He is also the God whose word can make life out of something that is dead. He's not only the God of creation; He's also the God of resurrection, and He has been anxious to step into your loneliness and create a love that is anointed by the very word of His mouth. God says that if you let some things die, if you turn away from them and put your hand in His hand, He'll lead you on to a blessing that He's already spoken into being.

One of the most amazing things to me about the mouth of God is that it is all-sufficient. Because He is life and He is His word, then His words are life. All I need in order to live is in God and in the mouth of God. So, when He speaks to me and tells me that He wants some things to die in me and in my life, I don't have to worry that His word won't be enforced; the word will do what needs to be done. Isaiah 55:11 says the word of God does not return unto Him void but will perform that which He sent it out to perform. Think about that. God's word will do what He says. He didn't say that Susie or Jack or Danny will do what He said. The very ability to do all that God commands is in the command itself. Why? I told you before that when God creates, He decides what something or someone is capable of. So when He gives a command, the power to do it is implied.

Our relationship with God, exhibited and expressed by His word, involves us, and it saves us. We are saved and sanctified by the very word of God who created us through His word. If you go to John 1:1 you will see that *"in the beginning was the Word."* You'll learn as you read further that the Word was with God, and that the Word was God, because the Word is Jesus Christ.

In Jesus Christ is the entire Word of God. He represents God's love for us. If you ever want to know God as more than a dark thundering cloud on a mountain, look at what He says through Jesus. There is no word more romantic than the Word that came forth through, in, and by Jesus. God spoke countless volumes to you when Jesus died for you.

God is a God who speaks, presently and continuously. He is never at a loss for words with you. First Peter 1:23 says we have been born again by the incorruptible seed of the Word of God, which lives and abides forever. That means the Word is continually alive in us and continually remaining or dwelling in us, throughout eternity. But it is also a seed. That means it needs to be planted, watered, and nurtured as it grows.

*Are you ready and able to hear what has come forth from the mouth of God?*

Matthew 13 says the seed was sown in you. The Word is in you. The question is not, "Is there a word from the Lord?" The question is, will you hear it? Do you want to hear it? Here's a better question: How's your heart? Jesus said that the condition of your heart is what determines your readiness and ability to hear what has come forth from the mouth of God.

The mouth of God is always speaking. It speaks to challenge you, encourage you, transform you, and comfort you. It speaks to every problem you have or every longing you could ever express (and some you haven't dared to). The mouth of God is God's declaration of His intentions toward you.

A while back my daughter brought a young man home to meet me. She had told me he was a preacher like me. He loved the Word like me. When I met him, I did what I always do when I meet the men my daughters bring home. I let him prove his intentions. Yes, this is the new millennium and we don't take a young man into the study for cigars to discuss "matters of the heart" anymore, but I still wanted to know what this man wants with my little girl. So I waited and allowed his actions to speak to me. One of the proudest moments of my life was having the privilege of performing their wedding ceremony. He had proven that his intentions toward my daughter were good, and I released her with joy.

I did not write this book to entertain you. I don't want to impress you or put on a show for you. I come as a sower who has been blessed with the privilege of sowing the Word of God. If you picked up this book and got this far, it was not by accident. God was not aiming at someone else and accidentally hit you. I don't believe you're interested in whether or not there is a word from the mouth of Kenneth Ulmer. If you are, you should know, my mouth can't create. My mouth can't save. My mouth doesn't sanctify or resurrect from the dead. I won't say that if you came looking for a word from me you came to the wrong place. You didn't. There are no accidents with God. I do have a word for you, but it's not from me.

# The Anatomy of God

God sent me to tell you that His Word, from Genesis to Revelation, is a love letter outlining His intentions toward you. In prayer and worship, God will emphasize and expound on certain portions and give you a chance to respond as a lover responds to the sweet things that are whispered in the ear. Oh yes, God will whisper to you. In fact, He's waiting for you to ask Him to leave that mountain and come speak to you.

Do you want to hear what He has to say?

## Seven

# Power toward Purpose: The Hand of God

Lord, I am willing
To receive what You give
To lack what You withhold
To relinquish what You take
To suffer what You inflict
To be what You require.
And, Lord, if others are to be
Your messengers to me,
I am willing to hear and heed
What they have to say. Amen.
—Nelson Mink, *Pocket Pearls*

There is probably no image—literal or figurative—no illustration, and no metaphor as multidimensional and complex as the one presented by the constitution and workings of the arm, hand, and fingers of God. There is no other part of the Almighty's anatomy that gives us as many nuances, as many facets, or as many glimpses into His nature, character, and motivation.

That's not surprising when you take a look at the human anatomy. The very structure of the arm is comprised of three large bones—the humerus, the ulna, and the radius—that work together to pull, push, pound, and perform just as the Father, Son, and Holy Spirit work in conjunction with one another. The hand at the end of the arm gropes, grasps, gives, and gathers while fingers fulfill the requirements of intricate toil and operation, intimate articulation, and indicatory expression.

As you move further down the arm, activity becomes more specific. Likewise, as you move down the arm of God to the hands and fingers, the functions become more precise and the objects more specific. Still, you have to understand that the arm, hand, and fingers operate as a unit. In Scripture, they are sometimes mentioned together, and often the concepts expressed by them are interchangeable. Regarding creation, for example, Jeremiah said, *"Ah Lord God! behold, thou hast made the heaven and the earth by thy great power and stretched out arm"* (Jeremiah 32:17). David looked at the same act of God in Psalm 8:3 as the work of God's fingers. When God sent a plague of lice upon Egypt, Pharaoh's magicians called it an act perpetrated by *"the finger of God,"* while God declared that *"the hand of the Lord"* was at work in His plague upon the animals. (See Exodus 8–9.) There are, however, some aspects of God's behavior that are specific to a particular part.

Although the arm, hand, and finger are all common biblical images of power, the finger, because of its relative size, carries with it the added connotation of authority. It was the finger of God that drafted the Ten Commandments on tablets of stone. (See Exodus 31:18.) Jesus, *"with the finger of God,"* cast out demons, which action proclaimed that *"no doubt the kingdom of God is come upon you"* (Luke 11:20).

A person in authority just has to crook a finger at somebody, and he will come. A parent can point at something, and a child will understand that means "pick that thing up and bring it here." My mother could point at me if I was misbehaving in church. Nobody saw that finger but me, but I knew it meant either straighten up or I would get it when I got home, or both! I wonder sometimes why my parents didn't point at me before I started acting up just to let me know they were watching.

The hand of God is unique in its depiction of God's possession or control of something. Implied in that image is God's authority. In fact, when Jesus declared in John 10:29 that *"My Father...is greater than all; and no man is able to pluck* [My sheep] *out of my Father's hand,"* God's authority is stated and assumed. But the main idea here is possession.

The consequences of sin force us under the controlling hand of God. Psalm 32 finds our boy David talking about what some scholars believe was his sin with Bathsheba. He said that when he kept silent about it, he suffered because, among other things, God's hand was heavy upon him. It is the picture of someone trapping you to keep you from moving, then pressing you until you cry "Uncle!" Except in this case "Father!" would have been more appropriate.

When you refuse to confess your sins before God, He will allow your sinful situation to hem you in and put the squeeze on you until you've had enough. Enough what? Enough pain, enough heartache, enough loneliness, enough shallow living, enough joylessness, enough dry, parched wilderness. David said his *"moisture"* turned to *"drought"* (Psalm 32:4). When you've wandered (or walked) away from the living water of God, He will let you get far enough out there, and then He will put His hand on you and press. And if you press long and hard enough on something that is dry, it eventually crumbles under the pressure. That's why David said in Psalm 51:8, in his confession and repentance of his sin with Bathsheba, *"Make me to hear joy and gladness; that the bones which thou hast broken may rejoice."* Did you get that? God broke the bones. The hand of God is a hand of giving and provision and kindness. But it is also a hand that can keep you from continuing in any direction that might destroy you. It is a hand of control.

Now, particular to the arm of God is the idea and image of protective comfort. It occurs whenever the arm of God is mentioned in the plural. The arms of God in Isaiah 51:5 bring justice to His people. And in Deuteronomy 33:27, *"The eternal God is thy refuge, and underneath are the everlasting arms."*

There's an old gospel chorus that declares,

> Leaning, leaning
> Safe and secure from all alarms;
> Leaning, leaning,
> Leaning on the everlasting arms.*

That is the picture presented here. When the arms of God have gathered you up and held you close to the bosom of the Father, there is nothing that can even come close to harming you. You can thumb your nose at the devil from the arms of your heavenly Father and say, "Na na-na-na na! You can't get me!"

Although the arm, hand, and fingers do illustrate particular aspects of God's nature, for the most part they are interconnected in form and function throughout Scripture, so we will look at them as a totality. In the three chapters devoted to this study, "the hand of God" will refer to the arm, hand, and fingers of God. Together, the three emphasize a variety

---

*"Leaning on the Everlasting Arms." Words by Elisha A. Hoffman, 1887.

of activities and attitudes concerning God. His is a hand of direction and a hand of discipline. It is a hand of provision and a hand of protection, as well as one that gives and one that guides. The hand of God speaks of the power of God. It speaks of the authority of God. The hand of God is rich with revelation about the character of God.

## The Hand That Delivers

The most vivid illustration of the hand of God in operation is found in Deuteronomy 26. Verse 8 of that passage says, *"And the LORD brought us forth out of Egypt with a mighty hand, and with an outstretched arm, and with great terribleness, and with signs, and with wonders."* Moses wrote that book of Scripture, and he said that God delivered them. He said God brought them forth. The *New King James Version* says that God brought them out and that He did it by His mighty hand and outstretched arm.

Almost every time you study or examine the story of Israel's coming out of Egypt, you will see a portrait, a paradigm, a pattern of salvation. In other words, the story of Israel's being redeemed and delivered out of Egypt in that day is synonymous with the deliverance we enjoy through our salvation by Jesus Christ. In fact, you'll often find references to Moses or Egypt in the New Testament when it talks about salvation that will take you back to this very incident. Then, and even now, the word *deliverance* conjures in the Jewish mind that specific chapter in Jewish history. So, when the apostles preached to Jews in particular, the parallel was very useful in bringing them to salvation. Today, that Old Testament record teaches us the eternal truths outlined in the New Testament. In other words, if we look at the hand of God and how it functioned for Israel in Egypt, we'll have a clearer understanding of how it delivers us even now.

Just as God's hand delivered Israel, it delivers us even now.

As we look at this episode in Israel's history, I want you to see how the hand of God is constantly referred to and its workings inferred in this passage.

> And the LORD brought us forth out of Egypt with a mighty hand, and with an outstretched arm, and with great terribleness, and with signs, and with wonders: and he hath brought us into this place, and hath given us this land, even a land that floweth with milk and honey.
> (Deuteronomy 26:8–9)

Watch the hand's functions. He brought us out. He brought us in. He gave us something. The Bible does not say that He sent us out or even, in this particular passage, that He led us out because both of those pictures give us the idea of a distant God. If God sends us out, it's like saying that He stays and we go. If He leads us, then He goes and we follow. You get the impression that He's up ahead of us and we're running behind. Certainly there are some significant images of that in Scripture, but here God says specifically that He brought them out, and He goes on to say that He brought them out by His hand. Then, the same hand that brought them out also brought them into the land that He had promised to them and gave them that very land as a blessing.

Now look at Colossians 1:13. That passage says that God *"hath delivered us from the power of darkness, and hath translated us into the kingdom of his dear Son."* That is salvation. God has delivered us from, out from, the power of darkness and translated or transferred us into the kingdom of His Son. One version says that God *"relocated"* us. The word literally means to take from one place and put in another place.

Here's what God is saying. When you got saved, when God "delivered" you, He took you out of the darkness you were in and placed you into the kingdom of Christ. You have to use your sanctified imagination here. He reached for you and

picked you up out of your "life before Him" and then trans-
planted you into "life with Him" through His Son. His hand
reached down into your darkness and lifted you out, then
translocated you. You see Israel and Egypt? That's "you" and
"darkness." He delivered you from darkness into the kingdom.

Whenever God takes you out of something, He only does
it in order to put you into something that's better than what
He took you out of. He never delivers you just to dump you
and leave you to fend for yourself. And He will never take you
from better to worse. If God has picked you up out of something and it seems worse to you, then He hasn't set you down
yet. He's just dusting you off. You didn't see all that mess in
your life because you were in darkness before. Once you're
in the light, you start to see all that He has delivered you
from. When He's done dusting, shaking, and wiping you off,
though, He'll set you down in something better than He took
you out of.

The problem many of us have is that we get so caught up
and wrapped up in what He's trying to take us out of that,
as soon as His hand gets hold of us, we slap it down or try
to reach back for what He wants to remove us from. We don't
realize that every time we reach back, we miss what He's got
for us on the other side. We're willing to settle for something
instead of something *more*.

Then there are those folks who are trying to get blessed
in the new kingdom while living by the rules of the old kingdom. Keep in mind that when God's hand deposited you into
His kingdom, that meant He placed you under a new authority. It's like changing jobs. If you were working for Xerox, then
got a job working for IBM, you won't get very far working for
IBM if your allegiance is still to Xerox. You won't last too long
if you're still trying to operate according to the rules and pro-
cedures of the old company. Come to church on Sunday—new

kingdom. Meeting that married man for lunch on Monday—
old kingdom. Praise God for the blessing of that new house—
new kingdom. Cheating on your income taxes to get the down
payment—old kingdom.

Too often we don't realize that whenever we are under the
authority of the kingdom of darkness, at best any blessings
we're receiving are just the devil's hush money. He's trying
to pay you whatever he can to keep you quiet about what's
going on in the kingdom of the Son of God. He'll give you just
enough to keep you satisfied and silent. He'll give you a little
of this, or a little of that, so that you won't focus your attention
on what's happening over in Jesus' neighborhood. He knows
that if you ever find out what God has to offer you in exchange
for your faith, you'll cut the devil loose in a New York minute,
make your way to the kingdom of light, and get your praise
on. Then the devil knows he's got problems. You see, it would
be all right if you got blessed and didn't say anything about
it. The folks over in the kingdom of darkness can't always see
you from that dark place. But if you shout loudly enough, they
can hear you. That's why you can't keep your praise to yourself
when God delivers you. And that's why God makes sure you're
so blessed with Him that you can't help but shout hallelujah.

## The Upraised Hand

The Bible says God brought the children of Israel out,
brought them to some land, and then gave them the land.
Deuteronomy 26:15 says, *"Look down from thy holy habita-
tion, from heaven, and bless thy people Israel, and the land
which thou hast given us, as thou swarest unto our fathers, a
land that floweth with milk and honey."* Get the scene. God's
hand brought them out, brought them in, and gave them some
land.

The land that He gave Israel was land that was promised to
them. In fact, it was promised to their fathers. The Word says

it was land that God *"swarest"* or swore to them. In Hebrew the word for swear is actually made up of two words. The first means to be lifted up or raised up. The second part is the word *ya*, which is the Hebrew word for hand. So when God is said to have sworn, it means He made an oath with His uplifted hand.

Before you testify in a court of law, you are sworn in. You are asked to raise your hand and solemnly swear to tell the truth, the whole truth, and nothing but the truth. The raising of the hand is really a tradition right out of Jewish culture. It is a symbolic gesture validating the oath or the promise being made. So the same hand that pulled Israel out of Egypt, put them in the land, and presented that land to them is the same hand that was lifted as a pledge to their fathers. God had made a promise to their fathers, which refers to the patriarchs Abraham, Isaac, and Jacob, and particularly Abraham because the promise started with him. The covenant God made with Abraham is first seen in Genesis 12:1–3:

> *Now the LORD had said unto Abram, Get thee out of thy country, and from thy kindred, and from thy father's house, unto a land that I will show thee: and I will make of thee a great nation, and I will bless thee, and make thy name great; and thou shalt be a blessing: and I will bless them that bless thee, and curse him that curseth thee: and in thee shall all families of the earth be blessed.*

Without taking the metaphor to a carnal extreme, try to picture it in your mind. God made a promise to Abraham, who was still called Abram at the time, with His upraised hand, for it is the upraised hand that binds the oath. God told him He would bless him and bless others through him. He promised to lead him to a land, give it to him, and make him a great nation, which meant that Abraham's seed became part of the promise. Abraham is long dead, but his descendants would receive the fulfillment of God's promise. Now look at Galatians 3:5–9:

> *He therefore that ministereth to you the Spirit, and worketh miracles among you, doeth he it by the works of the law, or by the hearing of faith? Even as Abraham believed God, and it was accounted to him for righteousness. Know ye therefore that they which are of faith, the same are the children of Abraham. And the scripture, foreseeing that God would justify the heathen through faith, preached before the gospel unto Abraham, saying, In thee shall all nations be blessed. So then they which be of faith are blessed with faithful Abraham.*

Let's take this a piece at a time. When God put you in the new kingdom, as I said before, you were placed under a different authority and therefore a different set of rules. Here God spells out the rules. In the new kingdom everything operates differently. There's a whole new system of currency. The things you used to negotiate and conduct business with before don't work now. It's not about your stuff. It's not about works. The Bible says the new currency of this new kingdom is your faith. The thing that moves things around, gets things done, and causes things to happen is your faith. God doesn't move the universe on your behalf because you're so good or because you're so cute. He doesn't help, comfort, guide, or provide for you because of who your mother and father were. He does it because of your faith.

God had Abraham's blessing all ready for him. And the Word says that because Abraham believed Him, which is to say he had faith, it activated the promise. And it was activated for Abraham and his seed. The faith of Abraham caused the blessing and promise of God to be passed down from one generation to the other. But the passage in Galatians says, *"They which be of faith are blessed with...Abraham."* In other words, the promise that was made to Abraham's seed will go only to those who have faith like Abraham. You may wonder what that has to do with you, since you probably can't trace your family tree back to old Abraham. What does a vow made to Abraham's seed have to do with you?

If you read a little further through this passage in Galatians, you'll find out that your family tree has deeper roots than you may have originally thought.

> *Brethren, I speak after the manner of men; though it be but a man's covenant, yet if it be confirmed, no man disannulleth, or addeth thereto. Now to Abraham and his seed were the promises made. He saith not, And to the seeds, as of many; but as of one, and to thy seed, which is Christ.* (Galatians 3:15–16)

Let's camp out here for a minute. God made a promise to Abraham and his seed. He didn't say *seeds* plural, but *seed* singular. Abraham has only one true seed, and that seed is Jesus the Christ. It is Jesus who was the fulfillment of the promise to Abraham's seed. Galatians goes on to say that it is because of God's promise to Abraham, fulfilled in Jesus Christ, that we are now in a position to receive the promise. Verse 27 says that we are sons of God through Christ, *"for as many of you as have been baptized into Christ have put on Christ."*

The word *baptize* means literally "to place, deposit, or immerse into." Sound familiar? Salvation took you from one place, which is darkness, and placed you into or deposited you into Christ. That is the hand of God at work. Having fulfilled His promise to Abraham through Christ, He now makes you a part of that promise by bringing you out of your sin, bringing you to Christ, giving you your land, which is eternal life, and keeping a promise He made to Abraham a very long time ago.

If you look back at verse 8 of Galatians 3, it says God told him that in him *"all nations"* would be blessed. That means it does not matter what the color of your skin is. God is bigger than your skin. It doesn't matter who your family is. God is greater than your lineage or your genealogy. He's bigger than your gender and your denomination. He keeps every covenant that He makes. And He vows in Galatians 3:29 that if you're Christ's, then you're Abraham's seed and *"heirs according to the promise."*

If I am in Christ, then I am Abraham's seed. And if I am Abraham's seed, then that means when God raised His hand and swore to Abraham, He was swearing to me. I now have the legal right and the divine authority to say, "Lord, whatever You said to Abraham, me too." God told Abraham it was time to move from today into destiny. Me too. He said, "I will make you a great nation." Me too. "I will bless you." Me too. "You shall be a blessing." Me too. "I will curse those who curse you." Me too.

I want you to see something here. The hand that brought out, brought in, and gave went into action after and according to the hand that was lifted in an oath. God raised His hand and made a promise; then He used that hand to carry out the promise that He made. You need to understand that the hand of God that delivers, provides, works, gives, moves, creates, and protects is first the hand that validated a vow.

Do you know why that first generation of the children of Israel was not able to go into the Promised Land? It was not because they didn't know the delivering, providing, guiding, and giving hand of God. It was not because they had not known the hand of His protection, His power, or His presence. It was because they didn't believe the hand that was raised in promise to Abraham. The people never had a problem believing that God could do anything except keep His word to deliver them into their land.

# Power toward Purpose: The Hand of God

Don't ever base your entire relationship with God on what you have seen Him do in your life or in the lives of others. Never forget that, above all, God is holy, uncompromising, unfailing truth. Hebrews 6:13 says that when God made a promise to Abraham, because there was nothing greater, He swore by Himself. In other words, God raised His hand to Himself and swore an oath to Himself. He was the One who vowed, and He would be the One who would enforce the vow. But that wasn't enough for the children of Israel. Is it enough for you?

You are Abraham's seed. Do you believe that? Will you stand on it before you step into all that God has for you? Will you believe it when you can't see your way? Will you believe it in spite of your current situation? You know God *can* do anything. So did Israel. That wasn't Israel's problem. Their problem was believing that He *would*. They questioned His integrity, His honor, and His very holiness. They received everything He mercifully gave them from His hand. But the hand that was raised with nothing in it but a promise—that hand they rejected. Have you done the same? Have you been content to accept everything God has in His hand but the promise you can't see?

We walk by faith and not by sight. And without faith, it is impossible to please God. So we walk; we move forward by pleasing God and not by what we see. Faith comes by hearing. What has God told you that you won't hear? It's what you won't hear that keeps you from moving forward. He made some promises to you in His Word. He vowed some vows to you. He raised His hand to you and said you were fearfully and wonderfully made. Do you believe Him? He raised His hand and said He would never leave you or forsake you. Yes, He chastised you, but before that, His upraised hand promised you that you were His son or daughter and that His chastisement would yield the fruit of righteousness in you. His hands knitted you together in your mother's womb. But He promised before that to conform you to the image of His Son and make you an heir with Him. Do you believe Him even as you struggle to look like His Son? Do you trust that the upraised hand of God means He will keep His word to you? Don't answer that too fast. In fact, let God answer it for you. Ask Him to show you what you believe and what you don't. What He says might surprise you.

## The Hand of the King

You will never grasp a clear understanding of the nature of God as it operates through His hand if you don't see that it is always a function of the sovereignty of God. His hand, more than any other part of His anatomy, is the most vivid illustration of it. The hand represents the outward appearance of the will. If you want something, I wouldn't know it until you reached for it. Even if you said you wanted it, your movement toward it is what proves your will.

The hand of God is confirmation of the will of God. Moreover, it is simultaneously a confirmation of the sovereignty of God. In other words, when we see the hand of God in action, it is always confirming what God wants, His right to what He wants, and His ability to get what He wants.

It is very important that you understand this. To say that your entire relationship with God depends on your understanding of this would not be an exaggeration. Think about it. The will of God is inextricably tied to the sovereignty of God. That means whatever God wants to do, He has the right and authority to do as well as the ability to do. So there is never any question that God will have everything He desires. The fact that He wants it is the guarantee that it will come to pass. Isaiah 55:11 tells us that God's word will not return to Him void, but will always accomplish what He pleases. His word is His will, and His will is always accomplished. And God is the only One big enough to say that, since He is the One who carries out His own will. He doesn't live by the rules. He *is* the rule.

Now, if you know what God wants, that means you know what's going to happen—no ifs, ands, or buts. If you know the will of God, you know that at some point in the future, His will is going to be done. That sovereignty is permanently affixed to the hand of God, and it is constantly affirmed and confirmed by that same hand. Knowing that, look at Deuteronomy 7:6–8:

> *For thou art an holy people unto the LORD thy God: the LORD thy God hath chosen thee to be a special people unto himself, above all people that are upon the face of the earth. The LORD did not set his love upon you, nor choose you, because ye were more in number than any people; for ye were the fewest of all people: but because the LORD loved you, and because he would keep the oath which he had sworn unto your fathers, hath the LORD brought you out with a mighty hand, and redeemed you out of the house of bondmen, from the hand of Pharaoh king of Egypt.*

This passage gives us a clear image of God's hand as it relates to His sovereignty. Usually, whenever God is speaking to Israel, you can assume the same principles and patterns apply to you. God said He brought you out of your Egypt because He chose you and loves you. God has sovereignly chosen you to be a people for Himself, a special treasure set aside just for His pleasure. He made a point to say that you weren't chosen because you're so great. In fact, you were the least. Then why did He do it? Because He loves you.

God's hand brought you out because His will desired it. He and He alone deserves credit for your deliverance. He didn't do what He did because of anything you did. His choosing to bless you was a sovereign choice *"because he would keep the oath which he had sworn."* So God brought you out because He loved you, chose you, and desired to keep the oath He made to Abraham. Now think. If the hand of God is an indicator of the will of God, and the hand of God was raised in oath to Abraham and by extension to you, then what does that mean? That means that God's oath was His sovereign choice.

Don't miss this. God didn't have to do anything He's done for you. He didn't have to promise you anything. He *wanted* to make a promise to you. He wanted to love you. His hands made you because He wanted to love you. You didn't make Him choose to love you. It was an act of His own will. God wants you to know that. He wants you to understand that. Everything He has given to you, promised you, protected you from, removed you from, and put you in was because He wanted to. He would have you to understand that His sovereign love means that He chose you, and He chose you because He wanted to.

Many of us have a problem with the sovereignty of God because it takes us completely out of the driver's seat. We can't do anything to earn God's love. We can't make Him love us more or harder or cuddlier. We can't control how His love comes to us. We can't control His choosing. We can't make Him "un-choose" somebody who hurt us. We can't force Him to choose somebody just because we like him or her.

*"Mighty hand"* in verse 8 speaks of the sovereign power that is in God, which in turn speaks to the fact that He decides to bless you. If you want to get technical, He decided to bless you before He even made you. The Bible says Jesus was the *"Lamb slain from the foundation of the world"* (Revelation 13:8). So your sin is not a surprise to God; before you made

the choice to sin, He had already decided to bless you with a Savior. He could have tossed you in the trash and made a new you, but He had already made a sovereign choice to make *you new* instead.

So He brought you out with His mighty hand. Take another look at Deuteronomy 7:8. It says the Lord redeemed Israel *"from the hand of Pharaoh king of Egypt."* Whenever you see the word *pharaoh* or *Egypt*, in Scripture, you can write "the enemy" in your margin. God said, when He sovereignly decided to bless you by bringing you out, He had to take you out of the hand of the enemy.

Remember that old kingdom of darkness from Colossians 1:13? Satan is the ruler over that kingdom. When you live there, you live under his rule and authority. But the Bible says God's mighty hand reached into satan's hand and took you out. You were in the enemy's hand. You were his possession. You were under his control. He was doing whatever he wanted to you, with you, and through you. And he was trying to block you from receiving the things of God and God's will for your life.

But God is sovereign, and His hand proved it and confirmed it by reaching into the hand of the enemy at will, taking your hand, and pulling you out so you could start living according to His will. He took His mighty hand, wrapped it around your little one, and snatched you out of that demonic hand that possessed you.

Now it says right there in the Word of God that you were taken out of the hand of the enemy. That means three things. First, satan's hand is just a hand, but God's is a mighty hand. Whatever satan wants to throw at you, God can block it or catch it and throw it back harder. When God gets ready to bless you, because His hand is so mighty, no other hand is able to stop Him.

Second, Deuteronomy 7:8 says that God's mighty hand pulled you out of *"the house of bondmen,"* meaning out of bondage. God knew where you were when He decided to bless you. He knew you were bound up and chained to sin. He knew you were in some mess. He didn't wait for you to get out of your mess to bless you. God doesn't bless perfect people. They don't need His blessing. He blesses only those of us who need Him to bless us. He blessed you by stepping into your bondage, your challenges, your trials, and your tribulation and taking you by your filthy, scarred, broken hand and bringing you out.

Third, and most important, if God took you out of satan's hand, the enemy had to know that you were missing. He had to realize that he had lost you. And just in case he didn't, David said that God is in the habit of making every one of His acquisitions very public. David said that when God blesses you, He prepares a table before you and throws a party for you. Now every party begins with a guest list. And this guest list is not complete until He invites all your enemies so you can sit down right in front of them as God blesses you. And He did it all just because He wanted to.

Don't think, child of God, that when you get plucked out of the hand of the enemy that the fight is over for him. I have bad news and good news for you on that front. The bad news is he still has a few tricks up his sleeve. The good news is they're still the same old tricks he's been using since Adam and Eve were trying to find some fig leaves to hide under. His strategy hasn't changed. He talks as much as he can, while he tries to shut you up.

When you're living in sin, the devil is real quiet. He wants you to make yourself comfortable with him, so he pretty much leaves you alone. It's not until he finds out that you've left him that his mouth starts going. He'll tell you you're not really saved. He'll try to convince you that any mistake you make will cause God to revoke His promises to you. He'll tell you to compromise, that God doesn't want you to be holy. After all, that's not realistic in these days. He just wants you to come to church on Sunday and be a nice person. If you're going to be married one day, it's okay to live together. Satan will use the mouths of the people closest to you to tell you that you've changed or that you're too judgmental if you tell them the truth about sin. Or he'll tell you that you're the reason you're so holy and anointed. If he can get you puffed up in pride, he won't have to turn you against God, since pride will turn God against you.

The best way to deal with the mouth of the enemy is to be ready with some words of your own—God's Word, in your heart and ready on your lips. When Jesus was tempted in the wilderness, He used the truth of the Scriptures against satan. Like Christ, you need to have a ready word in you at all times. There is something written in God's Word to deal with everything that could possibly come your way. Most people know that the Word is their sword. Don't forget it's also your shield. Ephesians 6:16 says your shield is your faith, but it is the truth of God through His Word that you have faith in. Imagine the upraised hand of God as your shield against every enemy.

*Imagine the upraised hand of God as your shield against every enemy.*

Every time you open your mouth with the truth of your testimony or the testimony of your faith, you do damage to the kingdom of darkness. Exodus 13:14 says you should be talking about it whenever the hand of God moves on your behalf. He says when your children come to you and want to know why you're offering your substance and your thanksgiving to God, you need to tell them, *"By strength of hand the Lord brought us out from Egypt."* God said that since He brought you out, you ought to have a testimony about His hand, and that testimony should be passed on to your children and their children. You never take credit for what God's hand has accomplished in your life. The text implies that when your kids get old enough to realize that they are blessed, when they realize that some of their friends don't live with the peace that they have in your home, don't tell them it's because mommy and daddy decided to give them a better life. Don't tell them it's because you pray, you tithe, or you *anything*. They need to know that the hand of God brought them the life they have. The hand of God bought the Air Jordans and the food in their bellies. The hand of God fixed the roof and paid the gas bill. The hand of God escorted them home from school when the boy down the street didn't make it past that drive-by bullet.

Don't you steal God's glory. Everybody ought to be able to look back at your life and point at some spots that are "nobody-but-God spots." I don't care how smart you are. There have been some things you couldn't think your way out of. There are some things you can't calculate your way out of. You may be driving a nice car now, but some of you remember your nobody-but-God bus pass. I like a good filet mignon, but I haven't forgotten my nobody-but-God baloney sandwich days. Nobody-but-God could bring you out of that mess you were in. And nobody but God is keeping you out of another mess.

My favorite nobody-but-God spot is the one that I remember in my prayer closet. Nobody but God

> Whenever you're faced with the mercy and grace of God's hand, accept it.

could love me enough to take off His deity and come into the filth and sin of this world to rescue me. And nobody but God would die for me for no other reason than that He simply wanted to. That's a hard one to wrap your mind around, isn't it? But let me offer you a little help. Whenever you're faced with the sovereign mercy and grace of God's hand, there's only one way to respond. Accept it.

He chose you because He wanted to. Accept it. He loves you because He wants to. Accept it. Accept His provision, His chastisement, His sunshine, and His rain. Accept the desert He leads you through and the oasis He will surely place in it for you. And how do you know that you have accepted God's sovereignty? Let me answer with another question. How much of your life have you thanked Him for? Your answer should be "all of it."

Acceptance is the proper response to the sovereignty of God demonstrated through the hand of God. And true acceptance must always come with gratitude. Now some of you might be thinking that you can accept a situation and not be grateful for it. That's not acceptance. That is tolerance. The two are very different. Tolerance affirms only God's power in a situation. Acceptance affirms God's entire person. Tolerance says you believe that only God has the ability to do what He's doing in your life. If you're not grateful, that means you think there's a better way than God's way. Acceptance says you believe that what He's doing in your life is the wisest, kindest, most loving, most perfect thing that could and should be done for you at that moment. And if that is true, you should be grateful.

I find it interesting that God tells us to enter His gates with thanksgiving. No one ever says thank you *before* he receives something. So the fact that God wants you to come to Him means His hand has already been active in your life. And you should be grateful.

Eight

# The Giver:
# The Hand of God

Daniel Webster was asked, "What is the greatest thought
that can occupy a man's mind?" He said, "His
accountability to God."
—Abel Ahlquist, *Light on the Gospels*

An idea has made its residence in my mind, taking up
space there like the smallest piece of exquisite furniture.
While other thoughts come and go, some welcome, some
not, this one has settled modestly within me. It doesn't have to
declare itself to me anymore. It is a fact of my very consciousness that appears with unwavering reliability at very specific
moments. When my son tells a joke, that tiny thought rides on
my laughter. It pulls the corners of my mouth into a sly, knowing
smile when I look at my beautiful wife. The privilege of preaching and teaching the Word is punctuated by it, along with the
majesty of creation, intimate friendships, the church I pastor,
and most of all, my salvation. The notion that so often adorns my
cogitation is simply this: God has given me so much.

That may seem obvious to some and trivial to others, but God is never more visible or tangible than when He is giving. He sees our needs and hears our cries. When the giving hand of God reaches out to offer provision, guidance, and comfort, He is revealing His compassion to us.

I struggle with God's giving hand at times, especially when I look at how much I have destroyed, squandered, and mis-handled of what He has already given me. So much of what I have represents second, third, and count-less chances. We used to have this thing when I was a kid called a "do-over." If you messed up at that game of rock, scissors, or paper, for example, you could say, "Do-over!" and you got another whack at it. The key was you were allowed only a cer-tain number of do-overs. After that, you had to live with your mistakes.

> The giving hand of God reveals His compassion to us.

Just when I think I've run out of do-overs with God, He has mercy on me and gives me another. Peter thought he ran out when he denied Jesus three times. But when Jesus forgave him and said, "Follow Me," that was a do-over. Saul was kill-ing Christians until Jesus met him on the road to Damascus, changed his name to Paul, and made him an apostle to the Gentiles. Do-over. The woman at the well, Ruth, and, of course, King David were all familiar with the do-over concept.

Does that mean we can do whatever we want to and God won't mind? Paul said God forbid we become presumptuous enough to take God for granted. Don't forget, the giving hand of God is also the chastening hand. When I was in school, my first roommate at the University of Illinois was a brother from a little farm town called Century, Illinois. He was a believer, and he liked to listen to country Western gospel music. He even got me hooked on it. One of his favorite songs was "May the Good Lord Never Show You the Backside of His Hand."

That's my prayer for you, and whenever you think about it, please pray that for me.

## Above and beyond Deliverance

When I look at the places God's hand has brought me out of and what it has brought me through, I think I would've been satisfied with deliverance. That was gift enough. But the giving hand of God never settles on just what you need. It goes above and beyond that. Remember, God delivered Israel with a mighty hand from the hand of Pharaoh in Egypt. They had been slaves for more than four hundred years. Simple deliverance would have been something to shout about. No chains and no backbreaking labor would have been reason enough to dance. But God's hand did more than just deliver. He did more than just move Hebrew bodies from one end of the desert to another. Look at Exodus 12:35–36:

> And the children of Israel did according to the word of Moses; and they borrowed of the Egyptians jewels of silver, and jewels of gold, and raiment: and the LORD gave the people favour in the sight of the Egyptians, so that they lent unto them such things as they required. And they spoiled the Egyptians.

Do you see that word *"borrowed"*? One version says *"asked."* Another says *"request."* The most accurate rendering of that word is "to demand" or "to demand the right to." It is a very strong word. You'll miss it in English. It is the idea of demanding what you have a right to. Moses and his crew went to Pharaoh and demanded a blessing. These were Hebrew slaves not begging, but ordering the Egyptians to hand over silver, gold, raiment, fine linen, and clothing. In this context of slavery, the emphasis is on boldness.

What made them bold? Keep in mind that they were not being brought out of Egypt because they were special in any way. They knew, and God confirmed it later, that they were not chosen because they were special, but because God's love for them made them special. There's the key. They were bold because of the God who was with them. The passage says God gave them favor *"in the sight of"* the enemy. The fact that He gave them favor in the sight of the enemy doesn't just mean that the enemy saw that they were favored by God. It actually means that in the eyes of the enemy, the children of Israel deserved favor from them. When the Egyptians looked at these people who were their slaves, they looked on them favorably. It wasn't because they were so wonderful to look at; it was because God had put His own favor in their eyes. They were looking at the slaves through favor-colored glasses, so they not only released them, but they also blessed them as they went.

Now in this scenario we see the hand of God giving favor to His people by putting His favor in the eyes of their enemy. Then He gave the children of Israel blessings of silver, gold, jewels, and raiment. Remember, these were slaves. In the Egyptians' minds the favor didn't make sense. (That's why a little later on, when they got a chance to think about it, they tried to come after their property—including the slaves—but it was too late.) Don't you know that when God gets ready to bless you, He'll bless you through folks who don't even know why they are blessing you? It won't make sense to them—or even you.

Some people are working at jobs they weren't qualified to get, much less keep, but the hand of God gave them favor. There were others with more degrees, more experience, and more talent than you, but God granted you favor. Their résumés are a mile long. Yours has three lines, two commas, and a period. But the blood of Jesus stamped your résumé "FAVORED," and it was moved to the top of the pile. Most of you think what you really need is a new job or a promotion.

No. What you need is the favor of God. If you have favor, you'll get the job.

You know you weren't qualified for that loan. That's why you got turned down so many times. But in God's timing and according to God's will, you got a loan because of God's favor. If I ever have a choice between the favor of God and a good credit report, I'll take the favor. I can handle the credit report if I have the favor of God resting on my life.

If you look closely at the passage in Exodus 12, you'll see the hand of God in another context. Pharaoh ruled the Egyptians, so that means when the children of Israel demanded to be blessed, they were making that demand to Pharaoh himself. The hardness of that man's heart was ordained and orchestrated by God. (See Exodus 4:21.) But Pharaoh still consented to release the slaves and bless them as they went. They had found favor in his eyes. That seems strange until you look at Proverbs 21:1.

> *The king's heart is in the hand of the LORD, as the rivers of water: he turneth it whithersoever he will.*

Pharaoh's heart was in the hand of God the way the rivers are. Rivers are different from other bodies of water in that they move from one place to another. They do not form themselves; rather, they are formed when outside forces act on them. Snow melts from a mountaintop, and over time the water, obeying the laws of gravity, runs down and cuts a river for the water to flow through. Eventually rivers empty into other bodies of water. The point is that the river is not in control of its beginning or its end. It turns and flows according to its origin and destination. Pharaoh's heart was subject to the hand of almighty God, so that when God was ready to grant His people favor, Pharaoh couldn't do anything but comply.

So we have the children of Israel, former slaves, leaving Egypt laden with silver, gold, fine linen, fancy clothing, designer gowns, and custom-made turbans. Psalm 105 says God brought them out with silver and gold, and it says, *"There was not one feeble person among their tribes"* (v. 37). They were not only delivered, but they also were healed and made whole. They didn't come out of Egypt moaning and broken. They came out strong and able so they could make the journey ahead.

God's hand had given them favor, then riches, and finally health and wholeness. They had been working so hard in Egypt that the Bible says they cried out, and their cries reached God in heaven. And these people, who had known nothing but backbreaking labor, were miraculously healed of every infirmity and disease. There were no achy joints, cuts, or bruises. The weak were strengthened and the lame walked. God knew the journey they were about to undertake, and He prepared them for it with health, healing, and riches—wait. Riches?

God knew the children of Israel were headed for the wilderness, yet He made sure that they left with silver, gold, fine linen, and raiment. They did not leave empty-handed. They left pulling carts and buggies and wagons full of silver and gold. Why? There were no stores in the wilderness. They carried fancy clothing, but there were no banquets planned for the wilderness excursion. Even today, there are no malls in that wilderness. What did they need with such wealth? They would be in the wilderness for forty years with no place to spend any of it. They didn't know they would be there for forty years, but God certainly did. The book of Numbers tells us that their clothes didn't wear out in the wilderness, so why did they need to bring all the luxurious linens and fabrics, not to mention the jewels?

God is not wasteful or frivolous. He did not give the children of Israel wealth to have a fashion show in the desert.

But He did give it for a reason that's outlined in Exodus 25:1–8.

> And the LORD spake unto Moses, saying, Speak unto the children of Israel, that they bring me an offering: of every man that giveth it willingly with his heart ye shall take my offering. And this is the offering which ye shall take of them; gold, and silver, and brass, and blue and purple, and scarlet, and fine linen, and goats' hair, and rams' skins dyed red, and badgers' skins, and shittim wood, oil for the light, spices for anointing oil, and for sweet incense, onyx stones, and stones to be set in the ephod, and in the breastplate. And let them make me a sanctuary; that I may dwell among them.

In the wilderness they were preparing to build a tabernacle as a dwelling place for the Lord. God told Moses to take up an offering to build His house. But how could poor former slaves be expected to give an offering? Remember all that gold, silver, jewels, fabric, and other wealth they left Egypt with? Here's the reason. So the hand of God filled their hands with blessings to the end that they would give some of it back to Him. Not all of it. Notice He said, "Take up an offering," not "Give Me back all the stuff I gave you." He could have. The book of 1 Chronicles says that when we give, all we have to give came from God in the first place. But there's an important principle here that most of us miss because we're so caught up in the stuff.

In the wilderness they were preparing to build a tabernacle as a dwelling place for the Lord. The riches they walked out of Egypt with would be used to do the work, as would the talent and time of the people. Exodus 35:10 called for the participation of every *"wise hearted"* person. The *New Living Translation* says every *"gifted craftsman"* was called into service, so it wasn't just about money. God was calling the people to give time and effort along with substance. I love how the verse says *"every"* skilled person among them should come and work. Most churches today are shorthanded because too many "skilled craftsmen" are warming the pews. God, though, called everyone who could come, to work. The Bible says in Exodus 35 that everybody from blacksmiths to seamstresses worked and gave so that the temple of the Lord could be built.

The people were not giving in order to purchase a blessing. They had already been blessed. They were giving to prepare for the revelation of the presence of God. God said the purpose of building the tabernacle was to house His presence. He wanted to dwell among His people, so He blessed them with the provision to build a place in which He could show up. Now get this, because if you do, you will never look at giving the same way again. God wants to be close to His people. That's how this book began, by explaining the desire of God to be seen by His people and with His people so that ultimately He can dwell in His people. First Corinthians 3:16 says, *"Know ye not that ye are the temple of God, and that the Spirit of God dwelleth in you?"*

The glory cloud of God's presence would eventually fill that tabernacle, and the people gave in order to prepare for that presence. Now if you want God to show up not just in your life but *in you,* you have to get a handle on giving. This is not a principle about money, though it certainly includes material things. But giving is never about what's in your hands. If it were, God would have told everybody, willing or not, to bring an offering. What He did was ask those people who were willing. Willing for what? Willing to see the presence of God.

Giving creates an atmosphere of revelation. It doesn't create the revelation, just the atmosphere. The giving does not make God come. Like I said, you can't purchase the blessings of God. But the offering prepares a place for God to come. The Bible says that when the tabernacle was finished, a cloud covered the tent and the glory of the Lord filled the tabernacle so that Moses couldn't even go in. God showed up, and Exodus 40:38 says, *"The cloud of the LORD was upon the*

Giving creates an atmosphere of revelation.

*tabernacle by day, and fire was on it by night, in the sight of all the house of Israel, throughout all their journeys."*

Every time I read this passage, it wipes me out. The purpose of their giving was not just to build a building. That was not God's end. The tabernacle was never an end unto itself. It was simply to be an accommodation for the revelation of the glory of God. That principle plays itself out throughout Scripture. For example, there was a widow woman in Zarephath, and that woman had barely anything to eat. In fact, she had just enough flour and oil to make what the Word says was to be the last meal for the widow and her son before they died. The prophet, however, told her to make a little cake for him first. If I had been that widow, I would have probably had a talk with that brother. I just told him I had only enough to feed me and my little boy, and he doesn't feel any shame about asking me to cut that in half, and to top it off, he asks me to feed him first!

But the Bible says she made the cake and gave it to the prophet, and then God showed up. How do we know? We know because the Bible says her flour and oil didn't run out for over a year. Supernaturally, every time she went to pour out some oil, there was more oil. Supernaturally, every time she went to get a little meal and thought she was at the bottom of the barrel, there was more meal. She gave what God asked for, and God showed up. Notice I said she gave what God asked for, not what the prophet asked for.

If you look at that passage in 1 Kings 17, you'll find out that the only reason Elijah the prophet showed up in Zarephath was because God told him to go there. And He told him there would be a widow there whom *"I have commanded...to sustain thee"* (v. 9). That word *"commanded"* doesn't mean that God had already told the woman to take care of the prophet. It is a word that means "appointed" or "ordained." In other words, God had already ordained that the woman would give Elijah what he asked for.

The hand of God has blessed you. And God has earmarked some of what He has blessed you with for you to give back into His hand. He has already decided where it should go and when. He knows what church you go to and who among your friends needs to be blessed specifically by you. He has given you time, talent, and treasure. His work is done. He has made you ready to give. Your job is to be willing. And when you give under those conditions, you can count on the blessing of His presence.

## It's about Revelation

All day and every day, the Lord was with Israel. But Israel never understood the principle that God had taught them about giving. They constantly turned away from God and gave their offerings to idols, and God would withdraw from them. They looked for the hand of God to rescue them, provide for them, and guide them, but they missed what God was trying to teach them through His giving. So often He would let them handle things on their own until that got them into trouble. Then, when they called on Him, confessed their sin, and humbled themselves, He would restore them to right relationship with Him. Still, they never got it, and God explained it in the book of Malachi.

> *"Behold, I send My messenger, and he will prepare the way before Me. And the Lord, whom you seek, will suddenly come to His temple, even the Messenger of*

*the covenant....Behold, He is coming," says the LORD of hosts. "But who can endure the day of His coming?...For He is like a refiner's fire and like launderer's soap....He will purify the sons of Levi, and purge them as gold and silver, that they may offer to the LORD an offering in righteousness."* (Malachi 3:1–3 NKJV)

Israel had always waited for the coming revelation of the Messiah. Malachi said He's coming. God said He's coming. He's preparing the way for Him to come, and then Malachi said some folks weren't ready for Him. It's strange how a blessing can turn into a curse. God said that the Messiah's coming would be a problem for some because they could not stand in His coming. When He comes, there would be a purifying going on that would separate the righteous from the unrighteous. God went on to say through the prophet,

*"I do not change; therefore you are not consumed, O sons of Jacob. Yet from the days of your fathers you have gone away from My ordinances and have not kept them. Return to Me, and I will return to you," says the LORD of hosts. "But you said, 'In what way shall we return?'"* (Malachi 3:6–7 NKJV)

Let's take this apart. God said that Israel was not ready for His blessing because they had not kept His commandments. In fact, the text implies that they had been repeatedly disobedient. This wasn't a one-time offense. Their sin was a lifestyle. It was their pattern. Now, normally God would have consumed them. He would have wiped them out. But He had made a promise to them long ago. He had raised His hand to them and made an oath. He had told them that they were His chosen people, and no matter how far they got from Him, as long as they repented of their sins and returned unto Him, He would not destroy them. He promised to restore their relationship with Him if they would return. So He said here, "You're lucky I'm a God who keeps His word and does not change. Otherwise, I'd be pouring out wrath instead of mercy, and you'd be toast." So He told them to return, but the text tells us that Israel didn't know how. They asked, *"In what way shall we return?"* Let's see God's response.

> *Will a man rob God? Yet you have robbed Me! But you say, "In what way have we robbed You?" In tithes and offerings. You are cursed with a curse, for you have robbed Me, even this whole nation.* (Malachi 3:8–9 NKJV)

This went right over their heads. Where did that come from? We were talking about being prepared. We were talking about receiving the coming Messiah. Weren't we talking about getting ready for the revelation of You, Lord, and how that revelation would usher us into a new dimension, a new elevation in Your will? We thought You were talking about a new unveiling of a part of Your divine purpose for us, so we asked You how we could be prepared, and Your answer is, *"Will a man rob God? Yet you have robbed Me!"* What is that about?

Stay with me here, because this is where communication between God and man usually breaks down. God says that you're lax concerning His law. You ask how, and God says something you don't want to hear or that you don't understand, and things get fuzzy.

Israel said, "How have we robbed You, Lord?" I love God. He's so specific when He talks to us, so that there's no confusion. Think about it. You can take something by accident. But you don't rob somebody accidentally. When you rob someone, you do it deliberately. God said they robbed Him. He didn't say they accidentally took something from Him or even that they mistakenly took something that they thought belonged to them. He said, "Israel, you robbed Me!" He didn't bite His tongue. He didn't stutter. He spelled it out.

He let them know that they robbed Him in tithes and offerings. Stay with me, because we're going to find out that this is not about the tithe and the offering. Remember, they began this conversation talking about Israel's readiness to see the revelation of God. He told them they were not ready. They asked how they could get ready, and He asked a rhetorical question to get them to see how serious this business of giving is.

When God said, *"Will a man rob God?"* that was appalling to them because here God was accusing them of something that could get them killed. He had just told them that the only reason they weren't consumed was because they were His chosen people. They did not understand that from the time the hand of God had brought them out of Egypt, He had put into action a spiritual cycle of preparation, expectation, and revelation.

They asked God how to receive His presence. He then told them what was standing in the way of it. He did not mention fornication. He did not mention adultery. He didn't say anything about backbiting or covetousness. He said the thing that made them unprepared was their giving. He told them that their giving was lacking, and therefore they wouldn't be ready to receive the revelation of Jesus Christ, the Anointed One.

Listen to me. They really didn't get it. I believe the text is not so much about rebellion as it is about a lack of understanding. It's not that they didn't understand that they had held back their tithes and offerings; it's that they didn't understand how serious their crime was. I don't say this to manipulate you or frighten you. And I will say again that this is not about your money. You can't purchase God's favor or His approval.

Why, then, is God's solution for Israel to give? He told them in Malachi 3:10 to bring the tithes they had robbed Him of into the storehouse. In order to understand what's going on, you have to look at the entire verse.

> *"Bring all the tithes into the storehouse, that there may be food in My house, and try Me now in this," says the* LORD *of hosts, "if I will not open for you the windows of heaven and pour out for you such blessing that there will not be room enough to receive it."*
>
> (Malachi 3:10 NKJV)

There's the pattern of preparation, expectation, and revelation. God said to bring all the tithes to the storehouse. The temple was maintained and the priests were fed by the tithes and offerings that were brought into it. If the people were not giving, the work of the ministry suffered. So giving prepared the house of the Lord. Then God said, "Give and expect Me to pour out a blessing you won't have room to receive." That is expectation. God tells you to bring your tithe and then expect Him to do some things. That's important because that expectation is your act of faith. *"Faith is the substance of things hoped for, the evidence of things not seen"* (Hebrews 11:1). When you give, God says you ought to expect Him to keep His Word to you about what happens when you give. He said He would pour out a blessing. That phrase *"pour out"* means "to empty out." God plans to keep pouring until the blessing He has for you is completely out of heaven and in your hands.

I love it when God said we wouldn't even have room enough to receive it. We can receive material things, so He can't be talking about that. The only thing God could pour out that we don't have room to receive is Himself. There's the revelation. The presence of God awaits any man or woman with a heart that is willing to give. Most of us look at this text and our minds automatically go to the tithe. But the grammatical

The only thing God could pour out that we don't have room to receive is Himself.

structure of the sentence suggests that the emphasis is on the giving. The word *bring* in *"bring all the tithes"* is actually the emphasis of the sentence. God wants you to bring to Him what belongs to Him, but you're blessed by the bringing, not by the tithe. He said the tithe is for the upkeep of His house, the house where He dwells with His people. The bringing is what causes the windows of heaven to open. How do we know this? The answer is in the question, *"Will a man rob God?"*

Remember, the problem is the robbery. That word *rob* means, in the original Hebrew, "to cover up something." Here's the idea. It is the picture of a person who puts his hand over the opening of a chalice or a cup to hide or withhold the contents. The people had robbed God by putting their hands over their tithes and offerings, which belonged to God. This was a serious offense. Hundreds of years later, the writer of the book of Acts showed us how serious.

The New Testament church was being formed, and, like the children of Israel, believers in that day were in a season of giving for the purpose of building the ministry. The Bible says the people were *"of one heart and of one soul"* (Acts 4:32), and they gave willingly wherever there was a need. But one couple got a little selfish. Let's look at it in the *New Living Translation.*

> There was also a man named Ananias who, with his wife, Sapphira, sold some property. He brought part of the money to the apostles, but he claimed it was the full amount. His wife had agreed to this deception. Then Peter said, "Ananias, why has Satan filled your heart? You lied to the Holy Spirit....How could you do a thing like this? You weren't lying to us but to God." As soon as Ananias heard these words, he fell to the floor and died....About three hours later his wife came in, not knowing what had happened. Peter asked her, "Was

*this the price you and your husband received for your land?" "Yes," she replied, "that was the price." And Peter said, "How could the two of you even think of doing a thing like this—conspiring together to test the Spirit of the Lord? Just outside that door are the young men who buried your husband, and they will carry you out, too." Instantly, she fell to the floor and died....They carried her out and buried her beside her husband.*

(Acts 5:1–5, 7–10 NLT)

You may think you're just affecting the church's account when you don't give, but it's much more serious than that. Peter said you aren't keeping anything from your pastor; you're defrauding God. He may not strike you dead, but there's a good chance that some areas of your life that should be flourishing may be dying. The violation of Ananias and Sapphira was not in the amount they gave. It was in their holding back something that belonged to God. They covered or put their hand over something that should have been given to God.

Obviously, when you put your hand over a cup, it keeps the contents away from others. But it also keeps anything from being poured into the cup as well. When you rob God, you keep Him from being able to bless you. He desires to bless you, but He can't because your own hand is in the way. That's why God said the people were cursed in Malachi 3:9. Part of His promise to His people was that He would bless those who blessed them and that He would curse those who cursed them. If you blessed the chosen people of God, you got blessed. If you cursed them, you got cursed. There's no in-between. There's no "option c," just (a) blessed or (b) cursed. How did this rule apply to the chosen people themselves? I just told you, there are only two options. In other words, when God's chosen people prevent God from blessing them, they are forcing God to curse them.

What God was asking Israel for was not money. Likewise, as you lay the pattern of God's command to give to your own life, your focus should not be on the money. But just in case it is, you should consider something. God didn't ask the children of Israel to give anything that He hadn't already given them to give. You didn't get that, so I'm going to repeat it. God did not ask them—and He does not ask you—to give Him anything that He didn't already give you to give. If you have ten dollars, He's not going to ask you for twenty. If you are a gifted singer, He's not going to ask you to devote your time to playing guitar in the church band. If you have no compassion in your heart, He'll do what He has to in order to give you compassion; *then* He'll ask you to give it.

We're so stingy with God, and we have no right to treat Him like He's making an imposition on us. We look at Him like we want to say, "What are You asking me for that for? Have You seen my bank account?!" I have news for you. He has seen it; and everything that's in it, He put there. If He asks you to give it, say you don't want to, but don't tell Him you don't have it. He can work on your heart if you're honest with Him. He can't when you look Him in the eye and lie.

God does not need your money, either. If He needed money, don't you know He can just make some? God will build what He wants, feed as many as He wants, and reach whomever He wants to with you or without you. He could build a ten-million-dollar sanctuary with twenty million people giving fifty cents apiece if He had a mind to. Don't think He couldn't. Some of you are wondering why, then, God talks so much about giving. And why does He command it as opposed to leaving our giving up to us?

Remember, the purpose of giving is to see the glory of God. When we give, God says we can expect Him to show up, and when He does, we'll see His glory. Where will we see it? In the temple. And we are the temple. (See 1 Corinthians 3:16.) Stay with me. God's goal is to dwell in the temple of His people. If God is dwelling in the temple, then He should be visible. In other words, if He is dwelling in us, we should look like Him. Our eyes should see like His do. Our ears should hear like His do. We should reflect His holiness. Our arms should be willing to reach out to lost souls, and *our hands should be giving like His hands.*

Hear me: hands that cover up what belongs to God do not glorify God. When God says, "You have robbed Me," He's not talking about money. He's talking about glory. God is a Giver. His love is expressed in giving. He so loved the world that He gave His Son. Then His Son gave His life for us. And we are told to give. Why? Because God desires to replicate Himself in us. Giving makes God visible to the world through us. That's why God loves a cheerful giver. He's a cheerful Giver. It is His pleasure to give to us out of His hand.

It took me awhile, but I finally got it. God doesn't want His money back. He wants His glory. God is a Giver of the most glorious kind. One of the most magnificent facets of His personality is His generosity. Because He has everything, can do everything, and is everything, there is no part of Him that doesn't give. He can't help it. In fact, God could not receive anything from us that would increase Him because He can never become more than He already is. That's important to know, since that means He doesn't need the glory we give Him, either. If we don't glorify God in our giving, He is no less glorious. If we do, He's no more. Think about it. Even the glory is for our benefit. He's not changed by it. We are. He only wants His glory for what it gives to us.

There's that thought again, flitting across my mind. God has given me so much. All that I have He has given to me. All I give glorifies Him but changes me, so all that I give gives back to me. Oh, that my hands would become the hands of God, anxious to give and not thinking too long on what is given back beyond how to transform it into another gift.

Nine

# The Potter:
# The Hand of God

Life is a grindstone. Whether it grinds you down or polishes
you up depends upon what you are made of.
—James S. Hewett, *Illustrations Unlimited*

O ne of the challenges of the ministry of the Word of
God that I constantly struggle with is the exhortation
and the declaration that Paul made in the book of Acts
when he said to the Ephesians, "I have not failed to declare
unto you the whole counsel of God's Word." (See Acts 20:27.)
We have, in our contemporary ecclesiastical settings, diluted
and diminished the Word of God to such a degree that we do
little more with our Sundays than play to the tickling ears of
God's people. The contemporary church has moved into such
a "bless me" mode that leaders are often fearful and certainly
hesitant to declare the whole counsel, in particular that part of
the whole that doesn't "feel good." Paul said to the Ephesians

that the record would show that he had not failed to say all that there was to be said, not just those things that the people would be comfortable with.

We have looked at the hand of God that blesses, rescues, gives, guides, protects, and keeps. Those images of God cause us to shout the roof off because they mean we are blessed, saved, receiving, secure, not lost, and not alone. However, there is another, not-so-comfortable aspect of God's hand that is difficult for many of us to deal with. Remember that the hand of God is inextricably linked to the will and sovereignty of God. What God wants, He can surely have. There is never a time that He desires something and cannot acquire it. And He doesn't possess anything that He doesn't want. That's because there is nothing that is out of God's control or outside His will—including us.

> The hand of God is inextricably linked to the will and sovereignty of God.

The hands of God are hands that shape and mold us and make us according to His will. In this context, we appeal to the Creator, the Craftsman, the Engineer, and the Designer in Him. Jeremiah 18 shows us God as the Potter, skillfully working out His will through a lump of clay.

> *The word which came to Jeremiah from the LORD, saying, Arise, and go down to the potter's house, and there I will cause thee to hear my words. Then I went down to the potter's house, and, behold, he wrought a work on the wheels. And the vessel that he made of clay was marred in the hand of the potter: so he made it again another vessel, as seemed good to the potter to make it. Then the word of the LORD came to me, saying, O house of Israel, cannot I do with you as this potter? saith the LORD. Behold, as the clay is in the potter's hand, so are ye in mine hand, O house of Israel.* (Jeremiah 18:1–6)

# The Potter: The Hand of God

Adelaide A. Pollard picked up the theme of Jeremiah 18 and said humbly and submissively,

> Have Thine own way, Lord!
> Have Thine own way!
> Thou art the potter, I am the clay.
> Mold me and make me after Thy will,
> While I am waiting, yielded and still.

God as a Potter is the picture of deepest intimacy and closest contact with the believer. His are the hands that handle us and therefore know us through the familiarity of touch. That can be a comforting image until we consider that the hands of a potter desire to go beyond tracing the outline and the shape of the clay as it is. The goal of the potter is always to change the shape that is there.

Likewise, the potter hands of God seek to change us into something besides what we were when we came to Him. This is where our discomfort begins—with the declaration of God that we are not what He would have us to be. I don't like hearing that. It messes with my ego. It deflates my opinion of myself. It pops the balloon of my pride.

When you buy clay from the store, it comes in a block—a nice, neatly packaged, pretty, sensibly shaped block. Some of you had built nice block lives, all neat and orderly. Then you found yourself in the hands of the Potter, and the first thing He did was pound the shape away. Nothing is neat anymore. That wonderful, clear, protective plastic has been removed and discarded. Your block is now an unattractive lump, and all things recognizable have been bludgeoned away by the fist of the Artist who has something in mind, but who hasn't bothered to inform you of what it is. Welcome to the hand of God.

There are two very important things you need to know as you seek to submit your intellect to the idea of God as the divine Potter. First, every artist knows what he's making before he starts working. It's important that you get that. God already knew His plans for you before His hands made contact with you. One of the first things God told Jeremiah was that his life was not an accident. His birth was not some fluke generated by haphazard human passions and proclivities. It was purposed in the wisdom of the sovereign mind of God.

> *Before I formed thee in the belly I knew thee; and before thou camest forth out of the womb I sanctified thee, and I ordained thee a prophet unto the nations.*
>
> (Jeremiah 1:5)

God is not trying to decide what He's going to do with you. He made you only because He knew what you would be. The hand of God is confirmation of the will of God. That means God willed you before He made you.

Second, you should know that God knows how to do everything He wants to do with you. That's just as important, but it's not always as obvious. Look at Jeremiah 18:4 again.

> *And the vessel that he made of clay was marred in the hand of the potter: so he made it again another vessel, as seemed good to the potter to make it.*

This verse grips me every time I see it, because it says the vessel that the potter was making was marred in his hand. Something doesn't sit right with me in that. It's the vessel the potter made. He made it. It's not a vessel he got from someone else's shop; the vessel was one that was made with his hand, and the verse says it was marred in his hand. It was flawed.

If it were on the side somewhere when it was marred—but that's not what it says. It might have made sense if someone else had made it and put it in his hand already messed up—but that's not what the text says. It says the vessel he made was marred in his hand. And when he recognized that it was damaged, he made it again into another vessel *"as seemed good to the potter to make it."*

The potter is identified as God. The clay is identified as us, believers, the people of God. The will, the design, the desire of the Potter is worked out on the Potter's wheel. This is our destiny. The shape of the vessel is God's will for our lives. But here is a piece of pottery that God made with His hands…and it's flawed.

The word *marred* means "not suitable to be used." It means "messed up." Here's a piece of pottery that is in the Potter's hand, and it is not suitable to be used. It's messed up. Marred also means "worthless, without value." There's some hope for somebody right there because normally if a potter made something that was flawed, he would cast it aside. But you don't have *a* potter working on you. You have *the* Potter working on you. The text doesn't say the vessel is cast aside. The text says that the Potter holds it in His hand.

Now the question I wrestle with at this point is this: what happened to the clay in the making process that marred it or messed it up? Did something happen to it in the making process that damaged it? Here's the Potter with a piece of pottery in His hand that He made that's flawed. That clay pot is us. The Potter is God. The Potter's wheel is God's method of expressing His will in our lives. When the Potter put the clay on the wheel and started to work, it was with His will in mind.

Watch this. He was making something. He wasn't just playing around with this clay. He was working intentionally and deliberately when He sat down at the wheel. He had an idea of what that clay would look like when He was finished working, so that His will would be manifested on the wheel. Let's jump down the road here, and maybe we can find out first of all what His plan was. What was the Potter thinking when

He got the clay? Go to Jeremiah 29:11, and let's at least get an understanding of what His will was.

> *For I know the thoughts that I think toward you, saith the LORD, thoughts of peace, and not of evil, to give you an expected end.*

One version says to give you *"a future and a hope."* Let's get that straight. When the Potter sat down at the wheel, the will of the Potter when He sat at that wheel was that the pottery He made would end up in a peaceful place. His thoughts of you, His ideas, His plans for your life are plans of peace and not evil. He did not plan and does not plan for His end for you to be evil, but that you would have hope for a future. Then what happened in the middle that caused us so much hell that we wound up in His hand marred and scarred?

Well, maybe He made it and put it down and something happened to it when He put it down. In other words, maybe He made it and something happened to it and when He picked it up again, it was marred. Something happened to it. Look at Psalm 31:5. It is a psalm of David, the words of which were also quoted by Jesus.

> *Into thine hand I commit my spirit: thou hast redeemed me, O LORD God of truth.*

David said, "I put my life in Your hand, Lord. I put my spirit in Your hand." That's a good place to be. Now what shape was he in when he put himself in God's hand? Verse 12 of that psalm tells us how he felt.

> *I am forgotten as a dead man out of mind: I am like a broken vessel.*

Another translation says, *"I am like a piece of broken pottery."* And another renders the phrase as like a *"discarded pot."* The meaning is clear. David felt worthless and broken.

He put his spirit into God's hand, and he felt like broken pottery. Don't move too fast through that. Have you ever felt broken? It seems like such a contradiction. David said, "I put myself in Your hand, but I feel like I'm nothing."

What has happened in your life that has made you feel worthless? What happened in your life that made you feel broken and discarded? Who damaged you? What happened that cracked your beauty? What marred your self-esteem? What devalued you? David felt like a dead man. He felt like he was going out of his mind. He felt totally forgotten and thrown away like a shattered vase, useless and worthless.

Life can break you. You will meet people day in and day out with smiles on their faces covering up broken and shattered hearts. I was in South Africa once, and I heard a report on the television that said South Africa was the rape capital of the world. At that time, there was a rape in South Africa every 26 seconds. Three out of four women there would be raped before they turned sixteen years old. South Africa is a country of broken women who have been abused and misused. What has broken you?

Sometimes you go to God even in your brokenness. Sometimes you have to go to Him with your wounds. Sometimes when you place yourself in His hand, you think that you are putting nothing in His hand because you feel like nothing. You look in the mirror and see nothing looking back at you. David said, "I feel like a broken pot." But even with his brokenness, David said, "I'm in God's hand."

I cannot tell you the number of times I have felt worthless. I cannot tell you the number of times I've felt like a failure, or the number of times I have felt useless. My only consolation was found in the knowledge that I was in His hand.

The Bible says that the Potter held the pot and that the pot was marred. We are never told what specifically marred the pot, but the next verse says that because it was marred, the Potter did something very interesting. The text says He made it again. Now in order to make it again, He had to put it back on the wheel. In fact, He would have had to crush it. It was already damaged, but in order to make it over again, He would have to reduce it back to the clay it was before it was pottery. Before it was a vessel, it was clay, and the Potter has to take it back to clay and put it back on the wheel to make it over again.

You're saying, "Wait a minute. I just went through something, and You're going to put me back up on that wheel? I've been through hell and high water and, in order to bless me, You're going to crush me? I already feel like I'm nothing. I feel worthless. I feel useless, and in order to make me over, You are going to start this process all over again?"

Remember Jeremiah 29:11. His plans for you are to give you peace and a future and a hope. That means that, as painful as things are, they will eventually lead to that expected end. The hands of God work only according to the will of God.

## A Battle of Wills

The damage done to the pot could have happened without the pot's permission. But there is another implication in this text that gives us insight into how the vessel was marred in the Potter's hand. The text suggests to us that the scars and the marring may not be because of what someone did to the pot, for we see that the clay has a will of its own and has the ability to resist the will of the Potter. As you continue to read through Jeremiah 18, you'll discover that the clay, God's people, have rebelled and disobeyed Him. So maybe we don't have to feel so sorry for every piece of marred pottery. If you keep reading, you find

> The hands of God work only according to the will of God.

that Israel had disobeyed God and that the marring of their vessel was related to their sin. The brokenness, the flaws, are a product of the choices they made. The Bible says they turned against God and, in so doing, they missed out on the blessings God would have had for them.

Fasten your seatbelts. We are in for some turbulence. God said that the nation had sinned, and because of their sin they were flawed and damaged in His hand. Here, then, where the Bible says that He would make the vessel over again, implying that He would have to crush it and break it, there is the implication that God is acting out of anger. The remaking of the pot is an expression of God's displeasure with it, and because He's not pleased, He'll make it over instead of letting it remain as it is. If it means a painful pounding down, then He'll do it in order to get what He wants. This is not the portrait of God's tender remaking or rebuilding. It is an image of His chastisement, which, while it is a function of His mercy and grace, is neither comfortable nor painless.

When you look at the text, you almost get the impression that Israel wanted to question God's right to make them over, for He said,

> O house of Israel, cannot I do with you as this potter? saith the LORD. Behold, as the clay is in the potter's hand, so are ye in mine hand, O house of Israel. At what instant I shall speak concerning a nation, and concerning a kingdom, to pluck up, and to pull down, and to destroy it; if that nation, against whom I have pronounced, turn from their evil, I will repent of the evil that I thought to do unto them. And at what instant I shall speak concerning a nation, and concerning a kingdom, to build and to plant it; if it do evil in my sight, that it obey not my voice, then I will repent of the good, wherewith I said I would benefit them.
>
> (Jeremiah 18:6–10)

God tells us that our relationship with Him is a two-way street. He says if those who turned against Him will repent, then He'll return to them and bless them the way He promised in the beginning. But if He declares a blessing and they turn away from Him, then they have forfeited all rights to the blessing. In essence, disobedience tells God that we don't want Him to bless us, so He withholds it. And He will chastise us until we learn to desire His blessing.

Let me tell you something about the hand of God. God loves you, but He will spank you. All you modern parents can't relate to that. God is not going to give you a "time out" in the corner. He's not going to wag a finger and talk to you. He's talked through sixty-six books' worth of Bible, sermons, friends, circumstances, and even directly to you in prayer. When He's done talking, He's done. And there's no use in your getting all bent out of shape about it. It's standard in your salvation contract. It's not even in the small print. It's right up under your nose. If you don't believe me, go to Hebrews 12:5.

> *And ye have forgotten the exhortation which speaketh unto you as unto children, My son, despise not thou the chastening of the Lord, nor faint when thou art rebuked of him.*

God is making something out of you. He's not playing around. He is serious as He labors and works with His clay. My concern is that many of us think that God is just playing. We come to church Sunday after Sunday and live any way we want to live Monday through Saturday. That's because we don't believe God is serious. Too many of us don't live our lives with the constant awareness that we are in the hands of an almighty and sovereign God. We go from one healing line to another, from one crusade to another, and between the crusades and the healing we live the way we want to. Some of us have "repented" of the same thing so many times that we don't even feel bad about it anymore.

Hebrews says that God is going to spank His children. And He says, "Don't run away when it's your turn." When it was time for us to get a spanking, my mother would wait in one spot. We'd run around the house and down the street, and she would just wait because sooner or later we'd have to come home. Then God says don't faint when He rebukes you. That's a strange one. I remember a time when Mama hadn't even laid a hand on my sister Kathy. She just drew back her hand, and Kathy started hollering. Mama said, "I haven't even hit you yet!" God hasn't even hit some of us yet, and we're ready to fall out. What are we going to do when He actually does make contact? The Scripture tells us not to fall out when God rebukes us and not to run away when it's our turn to get a spanking.

You know, discipline in our house was always made worse by the fact that we were forced to participate in our own pain. We had these trees in our yard, and when it came time for punishment, my parents made us go out and get the switch they were going to use on us. We had two trees. One was a willow, and the other one had long, thick, wiggly branches.

Mama would say, "You go get a switch." How cold-blooded is that? You had to pick your own instrument of destruction. There I was outside, pulling on branches from a tree, testing them for their pain potential. The problem was, you couldn't come in with something that was obviously not going to hurt you. I got more "double whippings" for bringing in little skinny wisps of willow than I'd like to remember. For a long time, I thought making me choose my own instrument of punishment was awful. I later found out that it was really quite godly.

Can you imagine God allowing you to choose your punishment? In 2 Samuel 24, David had sinned. He took a census when God had told him not to. The act was a signal that David didn't trust God and was checking to see how big his army was. God was not happy. He decided to punish David, but He made a deal with him. God told David, "I'm going to give you a choice between three punishments. Pick one, and I'll serve it up." That is the most amazing thing to me. David messed up; God knew he messed up. So God decided to cut a deal with him. It was multiple choice: (a) seven years of famine, (b) three months on the run from your enemies, or (c) three days of pestilence in the land. Then God said, "Let Me know what you want Me to do to you."

I would have said, "There has got to be a 'd' in this thing. Surely You can do better than that." I love David's response. David said, *"I am in a great strait"* (2 Samuel 24:14). The *New Living Translation* says, *"This is a desperate situation!"* Well, I guess so. But David's response was great. Here it is. He said, *"Let us fall now into the hand of the LORD; for his mercies are great: and let me not fall into the hand of man"* (v. 14). David figured he was safer in God's hand than he would be trying to deal with man in a famine or on the run. He chose God's hand. He knew it would be painful. He knew it would be uncomfortable. But he chose the merciful hand of God.

Here's what I want you to see. You have a choice. You've already made some choices that damaged you and marred your relationship with God. He wants to correct that. You can try to control your own life, try to fix your own messes, and leave yourself at the mercy of the world, or you can let the Potter put you back on the wheel and work on you. There have been times in my life when, just like David, I messed up. I've tried to run away from the wheel. There are times when I knew I was under the chastening hand of God, and I have learned to take Him seriously because I know that He is very serious about my sin. I learned to think twice about disobeying Him cavalierly or thinking that just because I got away with something once, I'm in the clear.

When we come to respect the chastening of God, He can then take us to another level of relationship. When you're a child, you are on your best behavior solely because of your fear of punishment. But God said that to fear Him is just the beginning of wisdom. That means there's another level. We have to get to the point with God where we resist sin because we know it disappoints Him.

> When we respect the chastening of God, He can then take us to another level of relationship.

Until I had kids of my own, I didn't understand when my parents and others would say that punishing their kids hurt them more than it did the kids. I used to figure my mother and father must have been in bad shape because they were wearing me out. Then I had children of my own, and I understood.

When my son Kenden was younger and he would disobey me, I'd spank him, but it hurt me. As he got older, the bond between us became closer, and discipline and chastening took on a new form. One time he got in trouble at school, and he came home crying. I hadn't even said anything to him, but he knew the school had called and that I was waiting for him at home. He came in crying, and he said, "Daddy, you're going to spank me, aren't you?" I'll never forget this. I was frustrated, and I was hurt. He was crying over what he had done, and I was so grieved over it I had a tear in my eye. I said, "Kenden, you have broken my heart. Daddy is so disappointed in you. Get out of my sight." I never touched him, didn't put a finger on him. And we were both hurting.

Do you know what your sin does to God? It breaks His heart, this God who has loved you, provided for you, prospered you, and saved you from so much. We choose to step out of His will, violate His laws, misuse and abuse ourselves and others, and all the while expect Him to bless us. Sin breaks the heart of God, and if you love God, it should break your heart when that happens.

The most amazing thing to me about the passage in Jeremiah is not that the pottery was broken or damaged, not that the vessel was cracked and bruised. It's not that at all. The most amazing thing was that, in spite of the flaws, the Potter continued to hold it in His hand.

That night before Kenden went to bed, he came to me, put his arms around me, and hugged me. He said, "Daddy, I'm sorry." No spanking, but pain. No restriction, but sorrow. No punishment, but repentance.

Have you ever had to go to God and say, "Father, I'm sorry"? Have you ever reached that painful place of holy contrition and brokenness, where you have to face the God who deserves nothing less than your best and say, "I did something that I know broke Your heart. I'm sorry. I did something with my body, Your temple. I'm sorry. I violated Your law. I stole from You. I won't forgive others. I'm sorry. I sinned. I'm sorry"?

The next morning Kenden got up, and, before he went to school, he came to me. He said, "Daddy, are you still mad at me?" I said, "Son, it's forgotten. It's over with. I love you." If we confess our sins, He's faithful and just to forgive us our sins and then cleanse us from our unrighteousness. (See 1 John 1:9.) That's what happens when we get back up on the wheel. That restoration is the work of the Potter.

Have you ever seen a potter work with a piece of clay? He is constantly dousing it with water to keep it moist and pliable while he works with it. Your water is the Word of God, and if you let God soak you with it and work it into you as

He fashions you into the vessel He wants you to be, you will glorify Him and live in the destiny He has planned for you.

## Unseen Hands

So far we have learned that the Potter has a will and that the clay also has a will. But there is one will that you might miss if you go by the passage too quickly.

Remember, the Bible says the clay was *"marred"* in the hand of the Potter. That could mean that the clay was acted on by some outside force. It could mean that the clay made some bad choices. And there is a third option. That word *marred,* when talking about clay, could also mean that it "contains foreign debris." It means there was something in the clay that was not put there by the clay, but it got mixed up with the clay and therefore marred the vessel produced with it.

The tenses of the verbs in the passage suggest that it was not the Potter who put the imperfections and the particles in the clay. In other words, the Potter is not to blame for the flaws. In fact, the voice of the verb could suggest that something happened to the clay.

As I said, there is the will of the Potter. There is the will of the clay. And there is the will of someone who did not want to see the will of the clay yield to the will of the Potter, so he exerted his own will and put a little something in the clay to make it resist. I want to suggest to you that the enemy also has a will and that he wants to put anything and everything and anybody in your life in order to mar and scar and deter you while you try to live your life on the wheel of the Potter.

It's hard enough being on the wheel as it is, but to be attacked and have stuff thrown into the mix puts us in an even more difficult situation. Sometimes the bad choices we make are the results of some stuff the enemy put into our lives before we were even born. He put it in our parents' lives, then they put it into ours.

That's not so far-fetched when you think about it. It brings to mind the parable of Jesus that likens the kingdom of God to a man who plants a field, and, while he is sleeping, the enemy comes and sows tares among the field. Wouldn't that be just like the devil? You're trying to be the best little clay you can be, up on the Potter's wheel, when something rises up in you that throws you off-kilter. Then, instead of making a smooth turn, you start to get all wobbly in the hand of the Potter. The next thing you know, He's pounding you down to an unrecognizable lump. But don't lose hope.

First of all, remember that you are on the wheel of a Potter who knows what He's doing. He knew the condition of the clay when He picked it up. He knew how much junk, debris, and foreign matter were in it. And when you started wobbling back and forth on the wheel, He was not surprised. You may ask, then, if the Potter knew the clay was that messed up, why did He decide to do anything with it? That is grace.

You are not who you are because you're so wonderful. You are who you are because the Potter knew what to do with you. You see all the mess inside. He sees His plans for you. You see flaws and scars. He sees a bride for His Son, pure and free from all the stuff the enemy put in there. You see what went into making the clay. God sees what's going to come out of His efforts on your behalf.

He put you on that wheel and let you go around and around. As you turn, He has His hands on you, molding you, caressing you, working you. His hands feel the bumps and lumps beneath the surface. His hands work the debris to the surface. He knows when to make you stand taller, and He knows when you need a good pounding down.

# The Potter: The Hand of God

There is a battle of wills on the wheel. It is the will of the Potter to bring forth a vessel that brings glory and honor to His workmanship. There is the will of the clay, and that will can choose to resist or yield to the will of the Potter. Then there is the will of the enemy, whose goal is to circumvent the work of the Potter by throwing as many things into the clay as he can.

Whose will is the strongest? The enemy would have you believe that it's either your will or his that is in control. If he can get you to believe that, then you will live the rest of your life at his mercy. The truth is, the enemy's will is stronger than yours—unless you surrender your will to the Potter. Think about it. If the clay continues to resists the hand of the Potter, eventually the Potter will remove it from the wheel, and it will dry up and become useless. But if you give your will to the Potter and stay on the wheel, He will work every scar and flaw out of you.

One of the steps in making pottery involves putting it into the oven to harden it. There's no way around it, child of God. You will see the fire. The enemy would have you believe that the fire can destroy you. However, let me tell you a little secret about making pottery.

It's not the fire that makes the pot firm. It's the architectural integrity of the pot *before* it goes into the flames that ensures its stability. If the pot was not made correctly before it was put into the oven—if there are air pockets or debris still in it—then the vessel will collapse under the pressure of the heat. Don't miss this. I'm about to give you a valuable weapon for your fight against the wiles of the devil.

When a potter puts a vessel into the fire, he is already sure it can take the heat. Let me give that to you again. The potter never, ever puts a piece of work into an oven until he is certain that it will not be destroyed by the high temperatures it will be exposed to. Now, certainty is relative. The potter can only be as certain as his own knowledge, skill, capabilities, wisdom, and ability to control outside factors. Who is your Potter? The last time I checked, He knew everything, could do anything, was perfect in wisdom and power, and nothing was out of His control. And He is the same yesterday, today, and forever, so I think He can be perfectly certain that if you have to go into the fire, you will be ready.

Some of you have been thinking that God uses the fire to find out if you can stand up in the heat. *He* knows you can; that's why He put you in it. He wants to show *you* that you can take it. Whenever you find yourself under pressure, in the heat, remember whose hands you were in before you hit the oven. Remember who shaped you and built you. Remember who knows you more intimately than you know yourself.

Don't try to get out of the fire before it's time. That is also under the Potter's control. His knowledge and wisdom are perfect. There are no hands more skilled than His when it comes to shaping destiny. Walking with God is constantly synchronizing my will with His will. It is having the desire to have only the desires that He desires me to desire. If He doesn't want it for me, then I don't want to want it.

Spiritual maturity is learning how to line up my will with the will of the Potter. That means submitting when my will is clearly different from His. That's when I have to practice my theology of "nevertheless." Every believer, in response to the molding and shaping of the hands of God, needs to have a theology of nevertheless. Nevertheless is that point where I say, "Nevertheless, not my will, but Yours, Lord." Anytime you ask God to let His will be done, you automatically petition Him to undo your own will.

> It is safer for you to be in the hand of God than any other place.

You're done asking if there's a Plan B; you're talked out, cried out, and run out. If there is another way, you don't want to know it. You just want to know which way He wants you to go.

Stay on the wheel. I promise you, it is safer for you to be in the hand of God than any other place. God is the only guarantee you have in this life. Anywhere outside of His will leads to destruction. Marriages are not made in bed; they're made on the wheel. Ministries are not built in schools; they are fashioned on the wheel of the divine Potter. Character, integrity, holiness, faith, long-suffering, wisdom, forgiveness, fearlessness, and love are all shaped on the wheel. Everything God desires for your life is on that wheel, and as with all things regarding the hand of God, the only right response is acceptance. Charles Swindoll wrote, "Acceptance is taking from God's hand absolutely anything He chooses to give us, looking up into His face in love and trust—even in thanksgiving—and knowing that the confines of the hedge within which He has placed us are good, even perfect, however painful they may be, simply because He Himself has given them."

"Behold, as the clay is in the potter's hand, so are you in My hand. Cannot I do with you as this potter?"

Can He?

## Ten

# Beloved Pursuit: The Heart of God

What does it look like? It has hands to help others, feet to hasten
to the poor and needy, eyes to see misery and want, ears to hear
the sighs and sorrows of men. That is what love looks like.
—Augustine

We've come to the end of our study of the anatomy of
God, and for all our tarrying in this examination of
the person and personality of the One by whom and
in whom we exist, we have arrived where we began: with the
heart of God. It is, after all, the heart of God that desires to be
known and moves heaven and earth to reveal Himself to us.

When we speak of the heart, various images come to mind.
We speak of the heart in very interesting terms, usually emotional ones. We seldom—sometimes, but seldom—think about
the heart in terms of the physical organ that beats in our
chests. Maybe we do during a physical checkup, but for the
most part we use it more often to refer to our sentiments, affections, and passions. It typically expresses how we're feeling.

The heart is the center of our desire, the seat of our will. To speak of a heart issue is to address something that goes to the very core of who you are. The Bible says a man is *"as he thinketh in his heart"* (Proverbs 23:7). Thinking is usually associated with the mind, but the writer of that proverb said that the real you thinks *with your heart.* Paul said it is with the heart that a man believes unto righteousness. He then went on to say that confession is made with the mouth unto salvation, but Jesus told the Pharisees that out of the abundance of the heart, the mouth speaks. (See Romans 10:10; Matthew 12:34.)

*"The fool hath said in his heart, There is no God"* (Psalm 14:1). The Word of God tells us that the person who believes that there is no God, who rejects the existence and personhood of God, is a fool. I'd call him a big fool, but the Bible just calls him a fool. We are to love the Lord with all our heart, meaning with our whole will and being. The psalmist prayed, *"Let the words of my mouth"*—but he didn't stop there; he also said, *"and the meditation of my heart"* be acceptable in God's sight because the heart is the center of who we are mentally, morally, and spiritually. (See Psalm 19:14.)

> The heart is the center of who we are mentally, morally, and spiritually.

Scripture employs various ideas using the heart. You consider in your heart. You know in your heart. You remember in your heart. A person having a special place in the heart speaks to your devotion to him or her. When you give your heart to someone, it means you love that person. You don't reach inside your chest cavity and grab a big, bloody hunk of cardiac tissue and offer it up to a person; it's a statement about your emotions.

The heart is the resting place for your joy and your courage. Pain comes into your heart. Desire, despair, sorrow, and fear all reside in your heart. In John 14 Jesus told the disciples that they shouldn't be troubled in their hearts at His leaving.

The heart is where our integrity is birthed and nurtured. It is where the real "us" lives. The Lord tries our hearts, refines our hearts, searches our hearts, and knows our hearts because that is where the true person lives. Where our treasure is, there will our hearts be also. There's a connection between our hearts and our treasure.

The other parts of God's anatomy have been anthropomorphic in their presentation. That is, they have been "in the form of man." We understand that God is a Spirit, but He speaks to us in terms we can understand and process cognitively. We have looked at the face of God, the ears of God, the eyes, mouth, arms, and hands of God. All those are anthropomorphic depictions of Him. When we look at ourselves, we can see these things on our own human forms. However, when we come to the issue of the heart of God, the representation is not so much anthropomorphism as it is *anthropopathism*. That is to speak of God in terms of human feelings as opposed to form. When we look at the heart of God, as with our hearts, we will examine it for its emotional facets.

God has an emotional personality. We've looked at some passages that talk about the anger of God and the joy of God. There are several passages in the Psalms that refer to God's laughing. God laughs. Imagine that. The divine, holy God actually laughs. It's interesting what He laughs at. He usually laughs at those people who think they'll get away with things. He laughs at them because He knows their just punishment is coming. He laughs, but if you read it, you don't find it that amusing. You're not always sure you don't fall into that crowd who tickles His funny bone.

> God has an emotional personality.

He is a God of emotions, and when we talk about the heart of God, we consider how He feels. He has a heart. What's interesting about that, and what actually surprises me, is not so much that He has one. It's the guy He picks to lift up as the example to those of us who seek to understand the heart of God. It amazes me. In all of Scripture, from Genesis to Revelation, from cover to cover, only one person is referred to by God as *"a man after mine own heart."*

He is found in Acts 13:22, where he is identified in Paul's sermon to the people at Antioch. There it says,

> *And when he had removed him, he raised up unto them David to be their king; to whom also he gave testimony, and said, I have found David the son of Jesse, a man after mine own heart, which shall fulfill all my will.*

The *"him"* who was removed refers to Saul, who was Israel's first king. When God removed him, He then raised up David, and He gave a testimony about him. He said that David was a man after His own heart. The people didn't say this. David didn't say this. God said it about David. He said, "I have found this man David." If you go back and read the context in which David came to be king, you'll find that there was literally a search. God actually searched, and out of all the people in Israel, He settled on David as the guy who is the kind of guy He's looking for. This is the guy whom God said was after His very own heart.

That is not said about anybody else in Scripture. The closest we get to it is in Jeremiah 3 where God said, "I will give you pastors after My own heart," but those were unnamed people. Here God went to great length to identify and spotlight David.

David the shepherd boy. David the king. David the giant-slayer, the great warrior, and the great leader in battle. David was God's man, called to lead God's people. David was the king who designed the temple, the very house of God. David, beloved of God. In fact, his name means "beloved." This is the man acknowledged by the Almighty as "a man after My heart." Here's the problem with that. If we were to take a poll and ask people what they remember about David, most of them—maybe not all, but most of them—would come up with a lot more than "he was a man after God's heart." Most of us, when we think about David, think about a different David.

David the king. Yes, he was a king. He was also an adulterer. David the warrior. Yes, he was that, but he was also a murderer. David was a great leader, but he was also a liar and a cheater. He was selfish. He was arrogant. He abused his power. He misused his position. He betrayed his friend and had him killed. Then he was involved in a conspiracy to cover it up. He was an adulterer. I don't know whether to scratch my head or shout. If this is the criteria God uses to pick His favorites, there should be a few more guys on the list.

I mean, a brother like that is absolutely amazing. This guy is the only one in Scripture to whom God gives that very personal endorsement. One writer said David was an insoluble enigma. He was an irreconcilable paradox. Holy man of God, yes, but with hellish ways. That will make you wonder, until you realize that if you focus on David, you'll miss the point completely.

The point in the passage is not so much the commentary about David's heart as it is a revelation about God's heart. In other words, if we make David our model, we'll miss it. Although he was the only one of whom it was said that he was a man after God's heart, if we make him our focus, we'll stay in our spiritual quandary. The issue is not that David had such a perfect heart, but that he had a heart that was running after a perfect heart. Go after the heart that David was after, and you'll be on the right track. David's goal was to access and acquire the heart of God.

Many of us make ourselves comfortable choosing role models and examples that we know we are better than. Some of us look at David and figure he's not so hard to beat. We may have done a little cheating in our lives, maybe even told a few lies. But come on. The man was a sneaky, cheating, lying, wife-stealing, murdering, arrogant, fornicating, manipulating, selfish hypocrite. Most of us aren't that bad. And we'd have a pretty good argument before God—if David were our model. But the emphasis is on the heart of God that David was after.

The story of David reads like a miniseries, and, if you deal with it honestly, you'd have to make that a cable television miniseries. Just the situation with Bathsheba is enough to warrant a parental warning or two. The G-rated highlights are these: David fell in love—no, it wasn't quite like that. He had an affair—maybe it wasn't even that. Let's just call it what it was. David saw Bathsheba and decided that he wanted her. So he sent for her, slept with her, and got her pregnant. Did I mention that David knew she was married to a friend of his before he sent for her?

Bathsheba was married to a brother named Uriah. Now, it wouldn't be so bad—it would still be bad, just not as bad—if David hadn't known that, but Scripture says he asked about Bathsheba and then sent for her. He knew who her family was and who her husband was. He slept with her, and she got pregnant. First David figured he would cover up his sin. He sent for Uriah, poor chump, who was out on the battlefield. By the way, that's where David should have been. The Bible says it was the time *"when kings go forth to battle,"* but David *"tarried still at Jerusalem"* (2 Samuel 11:1). It's that tarrying when you're not supposed to that'll get you in trouble. David was a king, but he had sent others out to fight for his kingdom.

When Uriah showed up, David tried to get him to sleep with his wife so he'd think the baby was his. That didn't work because loyal Uriah wouldn't think of sleeping with his wife while there were men out at war. Instead of going home to Bathsheba, he slept on the ground outside. That messed up David's Plan A. Plan B was even more cold-blooded. He sent Uriah back out to war with a note for Joab, his commanding officer. Of course, Uriah had too much integrity to read the note. If he had, he would have found out that David had ordered Joab to put Uriah on the front line of the most heated battle. David told Joab to make sure nobody watched his back and to let him get blown away. David wrote all that in a note, and he had Uriah deliver it!

Of course, Uriah got killed, David married his widow. This is a man after God's heart? There is something wrong with this picture. This is not a Kodak moment. But this is not about David's heart. This is about the heart that David is after. Stay with me.

God chose David. He is seemingly the most amazing choice imaginable in all of Scripture because of the negative things we know to be true about this man. We don't remember that he built great cities. We don't remember the design for the temple that God gave him. We are kind of like most people. We remember the bad things, the things that shock and appall us; the juiciest morsels lodge themselves in our mental archives. But God is not like us. God doesn't look at outward appearances. He looks at the heart. In fact, He said exactly that to the prophet Samuel just before He had him anoint a teenage David to be the future king of Israel. God saw something in David's heart. He saw something in his heart that appealed to Him. What did He see?

When you are studying Scripture and you want to get a deeper understanding or insight of a particular concept, idea, or word, there is a very useful hermeneutical tool. It is the law of first mention. When you are studying Scripture, one way to get a handle on a word or a concept is to find out when it was first mentioned in the Bible. If you can get some understanding as to how it was used the first time, it may help you with later references. So if we're going to understand something about the heart of God, it would be helpful to go back and find out when, how, and where Scripture first references God's heart.

### About God's Heart...

The law of first mention takes us back to Genesis 6. I'll give you the setting. We are preparing for the destruction of the world by water. We're in the days leading up to the Great Flood. God is about to open the windows of heaven and pour out rain for forty days and forty nights straight. Genesis 6 sets the stage for this period in the history of the world. It tells us why God is about to destroy His creation.

> *And God saw that the wickedness of man was great in the earth, and that every imagination of the thoughts of his heart was only evil continually. And it repented the LORD that he had made man on the earth, and it grieved him at his heart.* (vv. 5–6)

Where it says *"it repented the LORD that he had made man on the earth, and it grieved him at his heart,"* the *New King James Version* says, *"The LORD was sorry that He had made man on the earth, and He was grieved."* Verse 5 says something about man's heart. Verse 6 says something about God's heart. The chronology is significant. It's very important because the revelation about the heart of God in verse 6 is a response or reaction to something that is revealed about the heart of man in the verse before.

It says that God looked, examined, and saw the wickedness of man's heart. That word *wicked* has to do with depravity and destructive sinfulness. God looked at man, and He looked past all the fluff, past all the games, gimmicks, and facades. He looked past public images and checked out man's heart. It is a picture in our culture that would be like an X ray. God looked deep into the center of man, and He saw nothing but wickedness. To be accurate, He saw that the whole mind, heart, and consciousness of man, as well as all his purposes and desires, were consumed with, in, and by wickedness all day and every day. He saw utter corruption in the heart of man. He saw the antithesis of everything that He considered good, which means He did not see Himself in their hearts.

God knows that in order to get to know a person, you have to get to know his heart. Many of us make decisions, choices, and commitments based on the fluff, facades, and fronts that people put up to impress us. We are enamored with surfaces and trappings. Some of us need so much attention that we don't bother to go beyond the fluff. As long as somebody is validating or affirming us, we're okay. Flowers are good, and so are nice dinners. However, there is more to a relationship than flowers and food. You have to make sure that you get into the very core of who that person is before you commit your heart to him or her. You should know about his or her heart, not how good he kisses, how fine she is, or what kind of car he's driving. You'd better know who that man is under that three-piece suit, and you won't find that out by taking it off him. You have to know who she is without those fancy clothes, those acrylic nails, or those academic letters behind her name. You have to know who people are when nobody is looking. It's a heart issue.

When God saw the wickedness in the heart of man, the Word says He repented. One version says that God was sorry. Another says He changed His mind. There is a profound theological issue raised by this verse. If, as some translations imply, God changed His mind, how could He also be the God "who changes not"? He is omniscient, so how could He be sorry about something He created? How could the God in whom there is no wavering or turning, no shadows of changing—how can this God repent? To say that suggests that God made a decision and then reneged on it. It implies that something happened that God did not know was going to happen, and, when it did, He had to adjust His original plans. But if God found out something that He previously did not know, He could not be omniscient. How is it that God, who is omniscient, omnipresent, and omnipotent and is the same yesterday, today, and tomorrow, changes His mind?

First, you have to understand that the Word of God was not written for God. It was written for man, so everything in it is God's attempt to help us understand Him. As we study the heart of God, we find even here that it is presented to us in anthropopathic and anthropocentric terms; that is, it is in concepts and ideas that we can relate to. That said, when Scripture says that God changed His mind, it is an expression that helps us comprehend the seeming inconsistency between what He said at one point in time and what He said at another point. However, before that you have to appreciate the fact that something happened between verses 5 and 6 of Genesis 6 in order to unravel this theological conundrum.

God made a decision to create man and give man dominion over all things. Man rebelled. He changed and turned his heart against the things of God. When that happened, God responded with what appears to be an about-face. What you must always realize is that any consideration of the mind of God must include not only His omniscience, but also His foreknowledge. Foreknowledge means that, in addition to knowing everything, God knows everything about what's going to happen regarding everything He already knows. Therefore, when God makes a decision to bless man, He already knows how man will respond to it, and He already knows how He's going to respond to man's response.

When man responds as God knew that he would, then God moves to counter man's response. Because His nature is just, He cannot just ignore sin. When He sees it, He must respond in a way that is true to His character. What appears to be a change of mind, then, is in actuality God doing what He had planned to do all along. God knows what we're going to do before we do it, and He knows what He's going to do about what we do.

God planned to bless you, but He knew that because of your free will you would make wrong decisions and would disobey. He had already determined what He would do in response to your disobedience. He decided long before you were born what He would do to put you back in line so that He could bless you as He planned to all along. He loves you too much to leave you outside of His will. And He will do all that He has to do in order to get you back on track, including chastise you.

Chastisement is God's plan of pulling you off the road you're on, perhaps letting you cool your heels in a ditch for a minute, and then putting you back on the correct path of blessing. You have to realize, though, that He's putting you back on a path He knew you'd veer away from in the first place. So He has a blessing waiting on you when you get your bearings, but it's not a new blessing. It's the same blessing that He said He had before you messed up.

I told my son Kenden once, "When I come home, I'm going to take you shopping." Kenden wanted another pair of shoes. Kenden always wants another pair of shoes. But all such promises come with some built-in assumptions. There are always some unstated "givens" when parents make commitments. I came home that day to discover that Kenden had not done his homework. No homework, no shopping. That's one of those assumptions. He knows we don't go to the mall until all homework is done. Of course, he tried to cut a deal. "Tell you what, Daddy," he said. "Why don't we go shopping first, and then when I come back, I'll do my homework." Uh-uh. He got me with that one before. No homework, no shopping.

I went upstairs and about an hour later, Kenden came upstairs with a sheet of paper. It was his homework. He just said, "Can we go shopping, Daddy?" On the way to the mall, Kenden looked up at me and said, "I'm glad you changed your mind about going shopping, Daddy." When he disobeyed, it delayed his blessing. But I know my son. I wasn't surprised that he hadn't done his homework, and I knew that when he saw I was withholding his blessing that the homework would get done. When I went upstairs, I didn't change my clothes or take off my shoes even though I felt like getting in the bed because I knew I had to be ready to keep my word if he finished his homework in time.

To Kenden it looked like I had changed my mind. In actuality I was just delivering a blessing that was already earmarked for him before he messed up. It had his name on it. I just had to get him back on track first so he could be in a position to receive it.

God writes Scripture for our understanding, not His. It's hard for us to wrap our minds around omniscience. We have a tough time with foreknowledge. What we can relate to is what seems to be a change that, in the economy of God, is not a change at all but a manifestation of the continuum of His will, which comes out of eternity into time.

Just as significant as the concept of repentance in this passage is the actual definition of the word *repent.* It's much deeper than simply changing one's mind. It's a great picture word. It means "to breathe and to take in and let out a deep breath of pain." God saw nothing good in man's heart, and He let out a deep sigh of pain. He looked at His children and saw that every waking moment of their lives, every day, was taken up with thoughts and acts of wickedness, and His breath left Him in a painful moan.

Coupled with God's repenting is His grief. Genesis 6:6 says God was *"grieved in His heart"* (NKJV). That's like being stabbed in the heart. It is physical pain. Specifically, it means to inflict pain in the heart. To say that God was grieved in His heart speaks to the depth of His pain when He looked on the sin of men and the sin in them. Second, it speaks to the depth of His love for man that he could inflict such a wound on an almighty God. Here was man, created by God, blessed by God, raised up above all creation by God, made just a little lower than the angels, devoid of all the goodness that God had put into him. The sight of it pierced the heart of God, and He let out a sigh confirming the pain it had caused. The Scripture says man's sin was continual, habitual, and to the core. Man had taken everything that God had poured into him and defiled it, deliberately and maliciously. When God created man, He said that he was "good." He couldn't say that anymore. And at that point in time, God wants you to know that He was hurting.

I've seen that pain. I've stood at funerals with mothers who stood over the caskets of children who had broken their hearts. They had given all they knew to give, and their reward was rebellion. I've seen that pain. It's the pain that happens in you when you give your heart to someone and you trust him, support him, and count on him to support you and stand with you. Yet betrayal is the only answer you receive. He turns on you, and it gets so painful that you find yourself wishing that you had never let him into your life.

God was grieved in His heart when He saw sin. That fact brings us back to David. There's a clue there about David. The emphasis on the heart of David is not so much on the action of his sin but on his attitude about sin. David, being a man after God's own heart, is not to be seen in his disobedience or his rebellion; he is to be seen in how he regarded sin in his life. David had a sense of what his sin did to the heart of God. And the same feelings of sorrow and grief were duplicated in David's own heart.

*Do you have a sense of what sin does to the heart of God?*

God chose David and deemed him to be a man after His own heart before he sinned with Bathsheba. An omniscient God of foreknowledge chose David, so there was never anything David did that was a news flash to God. God knew that He had already put something in David's heart that would ultimately override and overrule the rebellion of his flesh. And so when David went to God after his sin, it was with the same pained heart that God Himself had.

David cried, "Have mercy on me, O God, not according to my own goodness, but according to Your loving-kindness, according to the multitude of Your tender mercies. Blot out my sin. Wash me, because I know I've sinned against You, and I know I've broken Your heart. I'm coming to You, Lord, because I need You to clean me up and fix my heart.

"I want Your forgiveness, Father, but I'm struggling because I also need something deeper than forgiveness. Every time I look at my life, my sin is all I see. I see stuff in my life that reminds me of my waywardness. I tried to do right by Bathsheba. I married her, but every time I look at her, I'm reminded of my crimes. When I look at my children, I remember the son who died because of me. Lord, my sin is ever before me. I've messed up. I've fallen down. I've blown it, and I've blown it big time. But there's something in me that wants to be like You. I want You to be pleased with me, but I'm so far from that right now. I need You to break the shackles of the guilt. I know what I've done to You. I groan with the pain of it. My heart is pierced and torn over my betrayal of You. Father, purge me."

Sometimes when you walk in sin too long, you begin to feel dirty. Your hands feel dirty, your feet feel dirty, your mouth is dirty, your mind has wicked thoughts. You try to do right, but every little thing that comes into your mind seems to distract you from the things of God. David needed to be cleaned up. He needed a bath. But he needed more than a surface cleaning. He had something going on beneath the skin. He had a heart problem. And David understood that the solution was not to scrub his heart clean; no amount of soap would do the job. The dirt was there from birth. *"Behold,"* he said, *"I was shapen in iniquity; and in sin did my mother conceive me"* (Psalm 51:5).

David understood that God wanted truth in the most inward parts of him. And he knew that simply cleaning his heart wouldn't do it. So he asked God to *"create in me a clean heart"* (v. 10). He asked for a brand-new heart. That word *"create"* means "to make or create from nothing." David knew he didn't have anything to give God to work with. If God were going to answer this prayer, He would be working from scratch. But David was a man after the heart of a God for whom nothing is impossible.

"Create a clean heart in me, Lord," was David's prayer. There it is. David asked God to give him a heart like His own. A clean heart is one that's pure. That's God's heart. A heart that's righteous—that's God's heart. David wanted a heart that was upright, innocent, perfect, and free from debris. That is the heart of God. That's what David was after.

What does it mean to be a man or woman after the heart of God? It means you respond to sin the way God responds to it. When He sees sin, He moves to remove it. You are a man or woman after God's heart when you move to remove sin from your life. Moreover, a heart after God's is a commentary on your attitude toward your attitude. How do you feel about how you feel about your sin? Genesis 6 says that every imagination of man's heart was evil. We can't just stop at what we do. We have to take active steps to abort sin before it is conceived in us. Sin is not born in our hands or on our lips. Sins that defile the body are not born on the skin. Our minds can be wicked. Sin is not just about what we do, but what we imagine doing. God sees beneath our behavior. He sees that ugliness we harbor in our hearts and hide from the world. He wants us to move to remove that.

Many of us want to condemn folks for what they do when the only reason we didn't do the same thing is because nobody asked us. We didn't get the opportunity, so we think that lets us off the hook with God. God says think again. He holds us accountable for what we wanted to do, what we imagined and thought about, that wickedness we rehearsed in our minds.

Fantasizing over pornographic material is not recreation. It is sin. You think what you do in the privacy of your own home doesn't matter? What about what you do in the privacy of God's home? *"Know ye not that your body is the temple of the Holy Ghost which is in you, which ye have of God, and ye are not your own?"* (1 Corinthians 6:19). You are painting the walls of God's house with sexual depravity, filth, anger, bitterness, unforgiveness, and envy when you allow those things to occupy your thoughts.

David said the only remedy is a brand-spanking-new clean heart crafted by God Himself, made from scratch. If we focus on David's sin, we'll miss the blessing of his character. Are we more sinless than David? That's like asking a woman if she's "more pregnant" than another. Sinlessness is absolute. You either is or you ain't, and all of us ain't. That's bad grammar, but it's good theology.

We could learn a lot from David. For instance, David kept very short accounts with God. When he saw sin, he didn't put off confessing it. When he confessed it, he didn't wait to repent. When he repented, he forsook it immediately. You don't see David doing the same thing over and over. And when he had confessed, repented, and forsaken his sin, David was quick to rejoice and praise God. In fact, he praised God throughout the whole process. There ought to be more Davids in this world.

## A Heart Unveiled

I want more than anything to have a heart like God's. I struggle with that every day of my life because I know that having a heart like God's is not just about what I do or don't do. It goes to what I think, need, and hide in the dark places of my consciousness. If I could just stop thinking about some things and forget others.... But like David, my sin is always before me.

I remember a song we used to sing in church that I still pray from time to time.

> Give me a clean heart,
> So I may serve Thee.
> Lord, fix my heart,
> So that I may be used by Thee.
> Though I'm not worthy
> Of all these blessings,
> Give me a clean heart,
> And I'll follow Thee.*

It's an odd song when you first think about it. I want God to give me a clean heart so I can serve Him. I want Him to fix me so He can use me. That makes sense, but then we jump to not being worthy of all the blessings. What blessings? The

---

*Margaret Douroux, "Give Me a Clean Heart."

blessings of serving God and being used by Him. If you're a man or woman after the heart of God, after a while, you'll stop asking for cars and houses, a husband or wife. There's nothing wrong with those things. They just won't be at the top of your prayer list.

The last two lines grip me. Give me a clean heart, and I'll follow You. How do you know when God is creating a clean heart in you? You'll follow Him. Not just to church on Sunday, but into eternity. You'll follow Him when it's comfortable and when it's not. You'll follow Him when your mother and father won't go with you and your friends talk about you for being "too holy." You'll follow Him when it makes sense and when it doesn't, especially when it doesn't.

You'll follow Him for one reason: you're after His heart. In Psalm 27:4 David said, *"One thing have I desired of the L*ORD*, that will I seek after; that I may dwell in the house of the* L*ORD* *all the days of my life, to behold the beauty of the* L*ORD*, *and to inquire in his temple."* We see David praying all the time in Scripture. He didn't make a move without consulting God. He praised God in prayer, interceded on behalf of others, repented, and petitioned. And yet here we find him saying he desired only one thing: to dwell inside God, to see His heart, to commune with Him, all the days of his life. That means every prayer, petition, praise, and plea of David was subject to that one desire.

When you're after God's heart, your desires get streamlined. If it doesn't bring you closer to the heart of God, you don't want it. And pretty soon you'll lose your taste for some things you thought would never leave you alone. Why? Because your life will become saturated and soaked in your need to see more of God. I want you to understand this. A heart after God's heart is not one without hopes or dreams. It is simply a heart that wants what God wants. Did you ever consider that you might be able to fulfill the desires of God's heart? Don't rush past that. "Lord, what can I do for You today?"

A miraculous thing happens when you sincerely seek to know the desires that reside in the heart of God. He tells you exactly what He wants, not in your ear, but in your person. When God reveals His wishes to you, they become a part of you. Remember, you are changed by what God reveals to you. That's why Jesus said abiding in Him meant that whatever you asked for would be done. When you really seek the heart of God, His compassion becomes your compassion. His yearnings become yours. You become what He wants. A person after God's heart cannot see the righteous forsaken or hear the cries of the oppressed and not respond. The heart of God breaks when it sees sin, not because of the offense, but because of the death that comes by it. Likewise, your heart will break when you see souls dying.

What does the heart of God look like? It looks like His eyes, which see every part of me and love me anyway. It looks like His mouth and His ears. I can see the heart of God in His hands as they deliver me, mold me, chastise me, and comfort me. His heart is the shape of His smile. The heart of God is God. And as I behold Him, my anatomy is transformed to reflect the glory of His heart within me. My eyes begin to see like His eyes. My mouth utters His words. My hands delight to do the things He would do.

The heart of God is God.

And what is the greatest desire of God's heart? That your anatomy would run after His anatomy. "Lord, what can I do for You today?" "Run after Me. Seek Me. Be curious about Me. Wonder about Me. Examine Me. Study Me. Look for Me. Look at Me. Want Me. Thirst for Me. Hunger for Me. Desire Me. Reach for Me. Come to Me. Grope for Me. Call out to Me. Listen for Me. Speak to Me. Turn to Me. Return to Me. Lie down with Me. Wake up with Me. Work with Me. Serve Me. Praise Me. Thank Me. Accept Me. Adore Me. Sup with Me. Drink of Me. Eat of Me. Enjoy Me. Inhale Me. Exhale Me. Live in Me. Die with Me. Love Me. Be loved by Me."

Be loved by Me.

Beloved by Me.

Beloved.

"David" means "beloved."

How do I know when I have found the heart of God? It's when I know, as David did, that I am His beloved; when I know, in my own heart, that I am unconditionally, unceasingly, relentlessly, intentionally, and unfailingly loved by the fathomless wonder of the heart of God.

# About the Author

D r. Kenneth C. Ulmer, who pastors Faithful Central Bible Church, located in Inglewood, California, is one of the most prolific and sought-after speakers of this contemporary age. Since his arrival at the church more than nineteen years ago, the congregation has grown from 350 to more than 10,000. Dr. Ulmer and the Faithful Central Bible Church are the new owners of the Great Western Forum, where they now hold their Sunday morning worship services.

In June 1969, Dr. Ulmer received his bachelor of arts in Broadcasting/Music from the University of Illinois. After accepting his call to the ministry, Dr. Ulmer was ordained at Mount Moriah Missionary Baptist Church in Los Angeles, California, in February 1977. In 1979, Dr. Ulmer founded Macedonia Bible Baptist Church in San Pedro, California.

Dr. Ulmer was called to the pastorate of Faithful Central Missionary Baptist Church in January 1982. His inexhaustible thirst for knowledge led him to continue his graduate work at Pepperdine University, Hebrew Union College, and the University of Judaism. In June 1986, he received a doctorate in philosophy from Grace Graduate School of Theology, Long Beach, California, which became the West Coast Campus of

Grace Theological Seminary. In May 1999, he received his Doctor of Ministry from United Theological Seminary.

Dr. Ulmer also holds an honorary Doctor of Divinity, which he received from Southern California School of Ministry, Los Angeles, California, in June 1989. He furthered his education by participating in the study of ecumenical liturgy and worship at Magdalene College at Oxford University, Oxford, England, in 1994.

He has served as an instructor in pastoral ministry and homiletics at Grace Theological Seminary, instructor of African-American preaching at Fuller Theological Seminary in Pasadena, and an adjunct professor at Biola University and Pepperdine University. Currently, he is a mentor in the Doctor of Ministry degree program at United Theological Seminary in Dayton, Ohio.

Dr. Ulmer has served as a council member of the California Attorney General's Policy Council on Violence Prevention, and a member of the board of directors of the Rebuild Los Angeles (RLA) Committee, designed to rebuild Los Angeles after the civil unrest. In 1994, he was consecrated Bishop of Christian Education of the Full Gospel Baptist Church Fellowship, where he also sat on the Bishops' Council. Dr. Ulmer has served on the board of directors of the Gospel Music Workshop of America, the board of trustees of Biola University, the Pastor's Advisory Council for the City of Inglewood, and the board of trustees of Southern California School of Ministry. He is a founding member of the King's College and the King's Seminary.

Dr. Ulmer's giftedness has also propelled him into the literary world as an accomplished writer. He is the author of two books: *A New Thing,* a reflection on the Full Gospel movement, and *Spiritually Fit to Run the Race,* a guide to godly living.

# About the Author

On March 17, 2000, Dr. Ulmer was installed as the presiding bishop over the Macedonia International Bible Fellowship, representing Zimbabwe, Namibia, England, Republic of the Congo, South Africa, and the United States.

Dr. Ulmer is a devoted husband and father. He and his lovely wife of almost 25 years, Togetta, have two daughters, RoShaun and Keniya, and a son, Kenden. They are residents of Los Angeles, California.

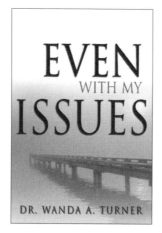

## ANOTHER POWERFUL BOOK
### from Whitaker House

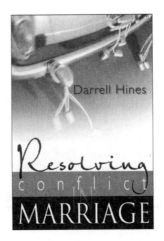

### Resolving Conflict in Marriage
Darrell Hines

Darrell Hines discusses the need for recognizing the spiritual forces that can affect your marriage. He identifies keys to preventing and resolving conflict, and how you can find a place of agreement and move on. Discover today how you can begin walking together in a new, stronger commitment that reflects godly principles and the true image of a God who is love.

ISBN: 0-88368-729-1   Trade   224 pages

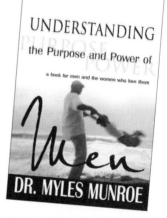
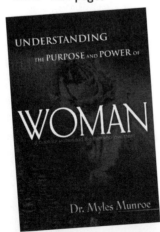